No Chariot Let Down

In Norton Paperback

*No Chariot Let Down: Charleston's Free People of Color
on the Eve of the Civil War,* edited by Michael
P. Johnson and James L. Roark

Black Masters: A Free Family of Color in the Old South
by Michael P. Johnson and James L. Roark

No Chariot Let Down

CHARLESTON'S FREE PEOPLE OF COLOR

ON THE EVE OF THE CIVIL WAR

EDITED BY MICHAEL P. JOHNSON AND

JAMES L. ROARK

W · W · NORTON & COMPANY

New York · London

First published as a Norton paperback 1986
by arrangement with
The University of North Carolina Press

Published simultaneously in Canada by
Penguin Books Canada Ltd
3801 John Street, Markham, Ontario L3R 1B4.

ISBN 0-393-95524-9

1 2 3 4 5 6 7 8 9 0

To our teachers,
Carl N. Degler
and
the late David M. Potter

Contents

Illustrations

Acknowledgments

Scholarship is a collaborative enterprise, and it is our pleasure to acknowledge that fact by recording our indebtedness to the men and women who have helped us prepare this volume. Archivists and librarians have made an immeasurable contribution. We have been the beneficiaries of the staffs of the South Carolina Department of Archives and History, especially Marion Chandler and Joel Shirley; the South Carolina Historical Society, especially Gene Waddell and David Moltke-Hansen; Special Collections, Robert Scott Small Library, College of Charleston, especially Ralph Melnick; the Southern Historical Collection, University of North Carolina, Chapel Hill; the Charleston Library Society; the Baker Library, Harvard University; the Yale University Library; the Library of Congress; the Friends Historical Library of Swarthmore College; the New York Public Library; the Pennsylvania Historical Society; the Public Archives of Canada; and the Archives of the Church of Jesus Christ of Latter-day Saints. We are particularly grateful for the invaluable assistance of E. L. Inabinett and Allen Stokes of the South Caroliniana Library, University of South Carolina, Columbia. Only those who have worked in this outstanding research library can fully appreciate Allen Stokes's extraordinary knowledge of its holdings, his ability and willingness to point scholars to promising collections, and his patience with those who continue to pester him long after they have left Columbia.

Several persons have graciously welcomed us into their homes and generously shared with us their knowledge of Stateburg and its people. Captain Richard and Mrs. Mary Anderson of Borough House provided us with several items from their family archives, and allowed us to spend a memorable day roaming over the former Ellison property, where the Ellison home and family cemetery can still be found. Mrs. Gery Leffelman Ballou and her mother Mrs. Pauline Leffelman recounted the discovery of the Ellison letters and life in the former Ellison house during the 1930s. Mrs. Julia Simons Talbert and Mrs. Emma Fraser told us of their memories of members of the Ellison family.

Many people provided assistance at various stages of the project. For practical arrangements, we want to thank John G. Sproat and

Bill and Hilma Wire. We are grateful to Rector Benjamin Bosworth Smith and Barney Snowden of Grace Episcopal Church, Charleston, for photographs and access to church records. Joe Reidy of the Freedmen and Southern Society Project shared with us his expert knowledge of the records of the Freedmen's Bureau, Washington, D.C. We also want to thank Charles Aiken, Lewis Bateman, Ira Berlin, Susan Bowler, Debra Busbie, David Carlton, Peter Colcanis, Jerry Cooper, Richard Coté, Carl Degler, Lee Drago, Gwen Duffey, Lacy Ford, George Fredrickson, Robert Harris, William Hine, Esmond Howell, Charles Korr, Cynthia Miller, Gary Mills, David Rankin, George Rawick, Loren Schweninger, Arthur Shaffer, Nan Woodruff, and C. Vann Woodward.

Our biggest disappointment was our failure to locate a single portrait or photograph of the Ellisons, the Johnsons, or any other of Charleston's free mulatto aristocrats. Their likenesses survive only in the letters themselves. For glimpses of the antebellum setting of places, objects, and white persons that figure prominently in the letters, we are indebted to Harold H. Norvell, Charles Gay, George Terry, and Chris Kolbe for photographs and to Karin Christensen for preparing the map.

Finally, we are grateful for the financial support of a Humanities Faculty Fellowship from the University of California, Irvine, and a grant from the Weldon Spring Endowment of the University of Missouri.

Abbreviations Used in Notes

CCL   Charleston County Library, Charleston

CLS   Charleston Library Society, Charleston

LC   Library of Congress, Washington, D.C.

PA   Public Archives, Ottawa, Canada

RSSL   Robert Scott Small Library, College of
          Charleston, Charleston

SCDAH   South Carolina Department of Archives
          and History, Columbia

SCHS   South Carolina Historical Society, Charleston

SCL   South Caroliniana Library, University of
          South Carolina, Columbia

SHC   Southern Historical Collection, University of
          North Carolina Library, Chapel Hill

EDITORIAL SYMBOLS

[unclear]   Brackets enclose a word (or words) in a manuscript
                 letter that we cannot read with certainty.

[*editors' notes*]   An italicized word (or words) enclosed in brackets
                 indicates the word does not exist in the manuscript
                 letter and was instead supplied by the editors.

No Chariot Let Down

James M. Johnson to Henry Ellison, August 20, 1860
Photograph by Charles Gay.

Introduction

In the summer of 1935, three little girls were playing under their house in Stateburg, South Carolina, escaping the hot sun and watching doodlebugs capture and eat ants. In the half-light Gery, Mary, and Francine Leffelman happened to notice a cardboard box toward the front of the house. When they crawled forward to investigate, they found that the box contained some letters underneath what the girls' father later identified as a saw from a cotton gin. The twins, Gery and Mary, had just learned to read and recognized that the letters were old. They took them to their father, Lewis John Leffelman, a forester educated at the University of Minnesota and Yale who had recently come to Stateburg to manage a large timber plantation. John Leffelman had always been interested in history, and he preserved the letters his daughters had discovered.[1] More than forty years later, in the spring of 1979, the South Caroliniana Library at the University of South Carolina acquired the letters from Mrs. Gery Leffelman Ballou. To bring those letters fully to light and to make them available to any interested reader, they are published here for the first time.

The letters are the correspondence of the extraordinary Ellison family. The patriarch of the family, William Ellison, was born a slave in 1790, but by the time of the Civil War he was the wealthiest free Negro in South Carolina and owned more slaves than any other free Negro in the entire South except Louisiana.[2] In 1816 Ellison bought his freedom from his white master (who may have been his father) and immediately moved from Fairfield District to Stateburg, a tiny aristocratic village about forty miles away in the High Hills of the Santee, some one hundred miles inland from Charleston. Ellison set up business as a cotton gin maker, a trade he had learned as a slave. Surrounded by the great planters and plantations of Sumter and adjoining districts, Ellison's gin business grew with the cotton boom until by 1835 he was prosperous enough to purchase the home of Stephen D. Miller, the former governor of the state.[3] Ellison lived in the house until his death in 1861. By then, although he remained a gin maker, he had himself become a big planter, making a hundred bales of cotton with sixty-three slaves on over eight hundred acres of land. Ellison's house, which still stands, remained in the family until

1920, and it was under this house fifteen years later that the Leffel-man girls discovered the letters.

The Ellison family letters are unique. They are the only extant collection of a sustained correspondence between members of a free Afro-American family in the later antebellum South.[4] All the letters were written by free persons of color to free persons of color.[5] James Marsh Johnson, William Ellison's son-in-law, wrote most of the letters, although letters from several other correspondents are sprinkled throughout the collection. Nearly all of the letters were addressed to William Ellison's eldest son, Henry. He lived in the family compound in Statesburg with his father, his sister, Eliza Ann (James M. Johnson's wife), his two brothers, William, Jr., and Reuben, and the senior Ellison's several grandchildren. In all there are thirty-seven complete letters in the correspondence: six are scattered between 1848 and 1858; twenty-six were written between November 1859 and December 1860; two were written during the Civil War and three others were written afterwards.[6] It is a commentary on the circumstances of the rest of the quarter of a million free Afro-Americans in the late antebellum South, on the vagaries of time, and on the long history of interracial suspicion, tension, and conflict that a meager thirty-seven letters to one free Negro family are the most to appear in the last century and a quarter.[7]

What the Ellison family letters lack in numbers they more than make up for in richness and historical significance. From the outset we could see that the letters were important, but we were not aware of their full significance until we had studied them carefully. The letters had evidently lain under the house for years and many of them were stained, the ink from one dampened page having blotted onto the next; others were faded, torn, or partially decomposed. Deciphering the letters was often difficult, but we eventually managed to make out almost every word. The full text of every letter written between 1848 and 1864 is presented here, with the few remaining illegible words noted.[8] Yet even after we could read the letters they were still difficult to understand, crowded as they are with hundreds of references to unfamiliar people, places, and events. Gradually, as we tracked down each obscure reference, a vivid and unparalleled portrait of Charleston's free mulatto elite came into focus.

The Ellison letters allow us to see the world of these free brown aristocrats through their eyes. All but four of the letters were written from Charleston, and the city figures prominently in three of those. The letters grew out of the family relationships that linked the Elli-sons to the highest circles of Charleston's free colored society. During the 1840s Henry and Reuben Ellison married daughters of the eminent free mulatto educator Thomas S. Bonneau; William, Jr., married a daughter of the prosperous free mulatto shoemaker John Mishaw; and Eliza Ann married a son of the well-established free mulatto tailor, James Drayton Johnson. By these marriages William Ellison's children linked the brown aristocracies of the upcountry and the lowcountry, just as young white aristocrats had done a generation earlier. The Ellisons were connected through the marriages to nearly all the other leading free mulatto families in Charleston: the Westons, the Holloways, the Dereefs, and others. All but two of the Ellison letters were written by members of this extended family network, and the family connection is evident throughout: gossip about kith and kin; expressions of love and concern; consultations about business matters; arrangements for loans, gifts, help, and visits; worries about sickness; and exchanges of news about church affairs, holidays, picnics, parades, and other public events. Family was the primary context of the daily lives of these people, and work, friendship, and participation in the larger society revolved around the family's needs and demands. In fact, most of the Ellison correspondence originated from a separation of family members that was the result of a decision to honor a familial obligation. Late in the fall of 1859 James M. Johnson left Stateburg, where he had lived since 1842, and returned to his native Charleston to help out in the tailor shop of his father, James D. Johnson, who was in his late sixties and, finding the work too much for him, was preparing to retire. From Charleston the younger Johnson wrote back to Stateburg to his brother-in-law and close friend, Henry Ellison.

In Johnson's letters the world of Charleston's Afro-American aristocracy unfolds.[9] Returning to the city of his youth, Johnson became the eyes and ears of the Ellisons, reporting on activities and events in the city with the wide-eyed curiosity and acute sensitivity of a man fresh from the backcountry. Although the Ellisons visited Charleston from time to time, they were tied to the routines of rural life, and they were eager for news from the homes and shops of the city's free colored elite. Johnson was well situated within the free colored community. His father was a member of the city's free brown aristocracy and a friend of many of Charleston's mulatto leaders. Having grown up in Charleston, the younger Johnson was known and trusted by his father's circle of friends. Johnson's letters, for example, contain information about all of the city's five wealthiest free colored families, and eight of the ten wealthiest. Several of them shared the Johnsons' trade and were among the most prominent free colored tailors in the city. Others Johnson knew from his activities in the Episcopal church, where they too worshipped. He saw others when they dropped by his tailor shop or when he circulated through the city on his rounds of visiting or attending to personal and family business. He wrote, then, with the knowledge of an insider. He was securely within the free brown elite, and, by virtue of his connection to the Ellisons and his father's established position in the community, he had access to its most exclusive reaches.

Charleston's brown aristocrats were skilled tradesmen—tailors, carpenters, millwrights, and others—and their families. They were a working aristocracy, an aristocracy with calluses. Their wealth was only a fraction of that of Charleston's white aristocrats, and, unlike the white aristocracy, it did not consist of lush tidewater plantations or gangs of slaves. Instead, it was largely in the form of urban real estate, an outgrowth of their quest for economic security. Many did own slaves, but usually only a few whom they employed as servants in their homes or laborers in their trades or workshops. Like most aristocracies, Charleston's free mulatto families were laced together by intermarriage. Lineage was of overriding importance to them because it was their lifeline to freedom. Because a child inherited the mother's status, ancestry set free people apart from slaves. Above all else, members of Charleston's brown elite were aristocrats because they were free, as the vast majority of Afro-Americans in the city and elsewhere in the South were not. In 1860, 81 percent of Charleston's 17,146 Negroes were slaves; in the entire South, 94 percent of all Afro-Americans were slaves; in South Carolina and the rest of the Lower South, slaves accounted for 98 percent of the Negro population.[10]

In Charleston and elsewhere freedom was associated with light skin. Mulattoes made up only 5 percent of South Carolina's slaves, but nearly three-quarters of the state's 9,914 free persons of color.[11] Charleston's free colored elite was uniformly brown, even though about a quarter of the city's 3,237 free Negroes were black.[12] While color and freedom distinguished Charleston's brown aristocrats from slaves, their property elevated them above most free Negroes. More than three-quarters of Charleston's free Afro-Americans were propertyless; only about one out of six heads of household owned a slave or real estate worth $2,000 or more.[13] Typically, members of Charleston's brown aristocracy owned both, as did some fifty-five individuals in 1860.[14] A little over twice that number owned one or the other.[15] In all, then, about 120 individuals constituted the core of Charleston's other aristocracy; including family members, the group numbered about 500. Something like 3 percent of the city's Afro-American population was an aristocracy of status, color, and wealth.

When Johnson returned to Charleston late in 1859, ominous clouds were gathering on the political horizon of free people of color. John Brown's abortive raid on Harper's Ferry in October raised once again the specter of free Negroes' making common cause with slaves and fomenting insurrection. Within weeks, legislatures throughout the South debated proposals to bring southern society into conformity with proslavery notions of white supremacy by eliminating all free Negroes, either by forcing them to leave or—the final solution—by enslaving them. In the North rampant anti-Negro sentiment helped propel the popular doctrines of free soil and free labor, the mainstays of the new Republican party. Scores of free Negroes in both the North and South concluded that there was no future for them in the United States and packed up and left for Haiti, Liberia, Canada, or elsewhere. Politically, times had never been so bad for free Afro-Americans.

In South Carolina the 1859 session of the legislature considered more than twenty bills to impose additional restrictions on free people of color, including enslaving them. Although none of the bills passed before the legislature adjourned, none had been rejected either, and all were available for reconsideration at the next session. Just before Christmas in 1859, Johnson sent his second letter from Charleston and congratulated William Ellison on the failure of the legislature to enact any of the restrictive laws. In one sentence he distilled the attitude of the brown aristocracy toward what was for most free Negroes the worst of times: "I prophesied from the onset that nothing would be done affecting our position."[16] This unflappable confidence that life would go on more or less as it always had and that the status of the free colored elite would not change endured through the spring of 1860, after the Democratic party convened in Charleston, split into southern and northern wings over the perennial issue of the appropriate protection for slavery in the territories, and accelerated the nation's skid toward war.

Johnson's early letters are significant precisely because they are filled with mundane, everyday matters. Despite harsh state laws on the books and harsher ones under consideration, despite the quickened pace of harassment and persecution of free Negroes and slaves, members of Charleston's free mulatto elite were not anxious nor were their lives severely cramped. Instead, their community was calm, even nonchalant, absorbed in the routines of work and family life, participating in revivals and May festivals, attending lavish weddings and receptions, observing courtships, savoring gossip about petty scandals, and traveling freely in and out of the state. The kinds of activities portrayed in Johnson's early letters are in fact hardly distinguishable from those described in countless letters written by contemporary whites. Within the context of late antebellum southern society, the lives of Charleston's free Afro-American aristocrats were remarkable because they were ordinary.

Although Johnson's early letters did not contain a hint of foreboding, events erupted in Charleston in August that threatened the survival of every free Negro in the state. Charleston authorities began to go door to door through the free colored community demanding unassailable proof of free status and proceeding to enslave those without it, sweeping up not only slaves who had enjoyed de facto freedom but also individuals who had lived all their lives as free people, some of them free for two generations. In the past the brown elite had remained invulnerable to the periodic crackdowns against free Negroes, but that was no longer true. The nightmare of enslavement and the politics that lay behind it caused a profound change in the outlook of the city's leading free colored families. Their confidence in the security of their freedom was shattered, and they began to despair. In December 1860, exactly one year to the day after Johnson had expressed his conviction that the position of free Negroes was safe from attack, he again condensed in one sentence the attitude of the mulatto aristocracy, revealing the change that had occurred in the previous few months. While the streets of Charleston still echoed with celebrations of the secession of South Carolina declared three days earlier, Johnson wrote, "Our situation is not only unfortunate but deplorable & it is better to make a sacrifice now than wait to be sacrificed *our selves*." [17] The enslavement crisis and secession forced the free colored elite to confront as never before the vulnerability of their freedom. Even those whose freedom was well established in existing law began to conclude that soon after South Carolina had left the Union, freedom for persons with any Afro-American ancestry would, one way or another, be outlawed. Beginning in August 1860, Charleston's brown aristocrats were preoccupied with the question of survival.

Until the Ellison letters became available, historians were entirely unaware of the Charleston enslavement crisis and its effects on the city's brown aristocracy and the larger free Negro community. Although it was a public event that involved hundreds of free people of color and many whites, although its effects were visible in the city for months afterward, the enslavement crisis had a secret history played out in private dramas behind closed doors in the shops and homes of free people of color. Johnson's letters disclose what happened in these quiet, confidential deliberations. Horrified by a crisis far worse than they had ever imagined, members of the free colored elite reassessed their situation and maneuvered to defend themselves. They deployed all their individual and community resources to protect their freedom and to survive. Using the network of kinship and association that defined their community, they took active steps to shape what their color dictated as their common destiny. They stood up to policemen and bullies; they called on the mayor and demanded that he quash damaging rumors; they kept in touch with the whites who remained their friends; they organized a petition campaign among Charleston's white aristocrats to oppose new proposals in the state legislature to enslave them or prevent them from earning a living; and they lobbied directly in their own behalf with influential, friendly legislators. Most important of all, they considered together what they should do; and that question quickly reduced to where they should go. "As it regards Emigration," James D. Johnson wrote Henry Ellison in mid-December, "your humble servt is on the alert with the whole of our people who are debating where to go."[18]

Many of their responses to the crisis of survival were rearguard holding actions designed to buy time for "our people"—the free mulatto aristocracy—to consider alternatives. Almost to a person they had concluded that in the newly independent South they would no longer be dark-skinned free persons but would be made light-skinned slaves. Escape from this fate, Johnson made clear, could only come through the combined efforts of the free colored elite. Slaves could dream of heavenly deliverance from their woes as they sang, "Swing Low, Sweet Chariot," and "Git in the Chariot and Ride Right Along." But the message of the spirituals held no attraction for Johnson. Like all God's children, free people of color were "free agents," Johnson wrote. A just God heard their prayers, but He expected them to act, to use their free agency to combat wickedness. Free people of color in Charleston could "not supinely wait for the working of a miracle by having a chariot let down to convey us away."[19] They had to save themselves.

Perhaps the most revealing disclosure in Johnson's letters is the sober self-interest that governed all the actions of the free colored elite. Their sense of security, so manifest in Johnson's early letters, was destroyed, but their confidence in their ability to negotiate their way through the most difficult circumstances remained firm. They retained their autonomy and their equilibrium. Although they were slaveholders, they did not identify with white slaveholders' quest for political independence. Psychologically, their sense of their distinctive identity remained very much intact. All their lives they had lived in a slave society that subjected them to special taxes, exposed them to humiliations purely because of their color, refused them equal rights before the law, restricted their opportunities for education, for worship, and for travel, and denied them all political privileges.[20] Many of these restrictive laws were enforced only sporadically, partly because rigorous enforcement got in the way of the smooth operation of ordinary social and economic activities and partly because the behavior of most free people of color did not seem to warrant constant vigilance. Still, the elaborate system of regulations confined most free Negroes to a constricted life of poverty and dependence, which led most whites to despise them as degraded parasites. Despite all these liabilities, a small brown aristocracy emerged and coalesced. The character traits that the brown aristocracy had developed and employed to prosper in such an inhospitable and unpromising environment—the self-discipline, the resourcefulness, the respectability, the shrewdness, the ability to decide correctly time after time how far to go without going too far—continued to serve them well during their survival crisis on the eve of the Civil War.

The antebellum achievement of the free brown elite was made possible by their success in sheltering themselves from the ruthless force of the law and in carving out a niche in what historian David M. Potter termed the "folk culture" of the South. Potter emphasized that personal, face-to-face relations played a crucial role in southern folk culture, imparting a distinctive style to social life that he termed "personalism."[21] Free people of color shared the personalism of the dominant culture; they understood it and they exploited it. In Charleston the mulatto elite established personal, face-to-face relationships with powerful whites—at work, at church, and in their neighborhoods. Leading white men were often the legal guardians of free persons of color and, in some cases, they were even linked by blood. Crowded together on the small peninsula, the white and free colored aristocracies intertwined. Although the bluest of Charleston's bluebloods apparently remained aloof, the mulatto elite maintained a vital personal relationship with powerful white men among the city's planters, lawyers, merchants, and bankers. Without this informal, personal nexus with influential whites, the mulatto elite would not have been allowed to build their substantial social and economic accommodations during the antebellum years.

Personalism was a fragile basis for security. It operated according to a fixed hierarchy and clear, though unwritten, rules. Free people of color might serve powerful whites in their shops and rub shoulders with them in the churches and streets of Charleston, but any deviation from the strict code of racial etiquette might be interpreted as insolence and invite swift retaliation. As long as free people of color stayed in their place, aristocratic whites did not consider proximity undesirable; in fact, they rather liked it since it facilitated prompt service from skilled artisans and reinforced their own sense of authority and racial superiority. But deference to whites was only a prerequisite for free persons of color to earn the benefits of personalism. Personal relationships across racial lines were impossible unless free persons of color possessed a set of traits usually subsumed under the term "respectability." The free mulatto elite had to work hard, to display decorum, piety, and sobriety, and to be reliable and loyal. To be guilty, or even to be suspected, of an action that would bring reproach in the eyes of whites threatened to disrupt these personal relationships. Above all, the free mulatto aristocracy needed to demonstrate repeatedly that, despite their Afro-American ancestry, they did not sympathize or identify with the plight of slaves and poor free Negroes. As long as they toed the line, they could expect white patronage and hope for white protection.

Johnson's letters contain numerous examples of the significance of personalism and of the ways it was consciously and carefully cultivated by the brown aristocracy. For instance, when Christopher G. Memminger argued against further restrictions on free Negroes in the 1859 state legislature and declared that from free Negroes "we are encouraged to look for everything becoming and proper,"[22] he spoke from personal experience. Memminger's home in Charleston was on Wentworth Street, just a few blocks from where Johnson lived on Coming Street. Memminger and his family were parishioners of Grace Episcopal Church on Wentworth, as were the Johnsons and a score of other elite free Afro-American families. Memminger may have patronized Johnson's tailor shop on King Street, as did other white planters, lawyers, doctors, merchants, and judges. Johnson and many other free persons of color were at least familiar faces to Memminger; they probably had a nodding acquaintance, perhaps more. In any case, when Memminger championed the rights of free Negroes before the state legislature, he was not defending strangers. He was personally acquainted with free persons of color who were decent, hard-working, useful members of Charleston's society. After the legislature adjourned, leaders of the free mulatto elite did not miss the opportunity to strengthen Memminger's regard for them. They went to see him, thanked him for his support, and subscribed to a gift for him. Of course, an exchange of favors that involved matters at the level of state politics was comparatively rare. The dense matrix of personalism was much more commonly composed of such things as one of the Ellisons picking up some cabbage seed for a white neighbor while on a trip to Charleston, or James M. Johnson gently teasing a white customer about "gallanting the Ladies," or a white merchant allowing Johnson to store his cotton seed free of charge. Such simple but all-important acts were the stuff of personalism, and they constituted the bonds of familiarity between the free mulatto elite and leading white families. They strengthened the brown aristocracy's confidence that their position was secure, and they reinforced the white aristocracy's conviction that it should be.

Within the social crevice shielded by personalism, the free mulatto aristocracy built a strong and cohesive community in the antebellum years. At its core were twenty or thirty tightly interwoven family clans. Overlapping these kin linkages and extending beyond was a network of religious associations and benevolent and mutual-aid societies. Membership in such organizations as the Brown Fellowship Society and the Friendly Moralist Society was restricted to men in the free brown aristocracy, and that same exclusivity can be seen in Johnson's letters. The vast majority of the city's Afro-American population, slave and free, rarely appear in the letters, and their problems or perspectives are seldom even noticed. Although the lower boundary of the elite community was not defined precisely, it certainly excluded most free Negroes and virtually all slaves. This made the general social position of the free mulatto aristocracy unmistakably clear: they stood between whites and blacks, between freedom and slavery, on what a young mulatto wheelwright characterized in 1848 as "a middle ground."[23] Their position on this middle ground was always anomalous, always contingent, always in tension with the law, always dependent on the sufferance of the white majority, always vulnerable to fluctuations in the political climate. To protect their terrain from the constant pressures upon it, the mulatto elite could not depend on the formal processes of law or on abstract principles of justice, but only upon the informal web of personal relationships, upon the affirmation by influential white aristocrats that individually and collectively free persons of color were respectable and worthy.

While personalism performed an invaluable function for the free colored elite in the antebellum years, it could not provide permanent security. As historian Carl N. Degler has demonstrated, there was no inviolable middle ground for mulattoes in the South.[24] Ineluctably, their Afro-American ancestry pulled them toward the status of slaves. Most whites did not see free mulattoes as a separate social caste but rather as light-skinned Negroes. The central axiom of the dominant racial ideology was that all individuals with any visible Afro-American ancestry should be slaves, for their own good and for that of the South as a whole. As the white South moved toward secession, the brown aristocracy's middle ground progressively narrowed and tilted ever more steeply toward slavery. On the eve of disunion, politics in South Carolina strained the ties of personalism. In the August enslavement crisis few white aristocrats stepped forward to defend free Negroes. The carefully tended relationships of patronage proved so ineffective that the free colored elite concluded that survival required emigration. Politics overpowered the informal bonds of personalism because the white friends of Charleston's brown elite were outnumbered by whites inside and outside of the city who had anything but a valued personal relationship with free Negroes.

In Charleston a rapidly expanding white working class resented the personal relationships that bound free Negroes and white aristocrats. Often, white craftsmen competed for work with free colored tradesmen; many other white workingmen struggled along at lesser jobs, more in competition with slaves than free Negroes. To these whites the ideology of white supremacy was alluring and its implications were clear. They bristled at the relative prosperity of the free colored elite, who were far better off than most white workingmen. They were galled when free persons of color were favored by white aristocrats with a contract for work or a sociable conversation. The deportment and appearance of free persons of color that so impressed white aristocrats appeared to white workingmen as ridiculous pretension and overweening arrogance. During the 1850s the number of working-class whites in Charleston grew, and by 1860 the city contained a white majority for the first time in its history. As their numbers grew, their political leverage increased accordingly. White workingmen were largely responsible for precipitating the enslavement crisis, and their influence continued to be crucial in subsequent months as they elected representatives to the state legislature pledged to eliminate free colored competition once and for all.

Free Negroes were also under attack outside Charleston. The city contained only 6 percent of the state's total population, but it housed fully one-third of the state's free people of color. Away from the city, free Negroes were widely scattered and almost entirely incapable of sustaining a full-scale community. Unlike the Ellisons, who were in so many ways exceptional, almost all rural free Negroes found it impossible to attain elite status. Most eked out a living as best they could, working as laborers at whatever they could find. Opportunities of all kinds—for work, education, community—were slim, and the free colored community of Charleston was too far away and too refined to be readily accessible. By default, the social network of rural free Negroes often included slaves, as friends, as co-workers, and as relatives. Many rural free Negroes were themselves not far removed from slavery, either in the date of their manumission or in their living conditions. Upcountry planters typically looked upon free Negroes as ill-disciplined rogues, likely to steal corn and livestock and to set a bad example for slaves by their free, idle, dissolute existence. Ultimately, upcountry whites believed, free people of color subverted the racial subordination that was the essence of slavery. Nothing would be lost and much would be gained, their representatives argued in the state legislature, if freedom were prohibited to all Negroes.

During the secession crisis free Afro-Americans in South Carolina encountered a dangerous new balance of political forces. Their enemies among upcountry planters and Charleston's white workingmen were united in their demands for extreme measures to repress, eliminate, or enslave all free Negroes. Their aristocratic white friends in Charleston were not only outnumbered but also, as the state edged closer to secession, were drawn by their fealty to slavery and white supremacy to seek a united front with the white majority as the surest security in the uncertain times ahead. Conflict between whites in Charleston, in the state, and in the nation loosened the bonds of personalism, separated the brown aristocrats from their friends, and exposed them to their enemies. The protective strategy they had followed so carefully for so many years was bankrupt. Upright behavior, hard work, the ownership of property and even of slaves had failed to secure their freedom. The middle ground on which they had lived and prospered for decades began to slip away as they were pulled from their unique status by their race. In the crisis of survival, the only thing Charleston's free mulattoes had left to depend upon was themselves.

In the months between the August enslavement crisis and the firing on Fort Sumter the following April, hundreds of free people of color in Charleston packed up what belongings they could take with them, sold the rest for whatever they could get, assembled their families, and emigrated from the city. But most of the members of the free mulatto elite did not leave, despite their decision to do so.

Unable to bring themselves to walk away from their accomplishments, they became trapped by the depreciated value of their property, the business standstill brought on by secession, and by the increasing difficulty of getting safe passage out of the state. Even more important, they were ever watchful for opportunities to piece things back together, to reestablish their personal connections to powerful whites who valued and trusted them. Through their own efforts and because the war forced white South Carolinians to look elsewhere, they survived the war. Several were among the most important leaders during the era of Reconstruction.[25] In Johnson's letters the longevity and durability of the mulatto elite are cast in a new light. Their loyalty to the South, to the Confederacy, and to slavery was never unconditional. As always, their loyalty turned on their ability to maintain and protect their own freedom.

In transcribing and publishing the letters we wanted to remain faithful to the originals and at the same time to make them accessible to a modern reader. These aims are somewhat contradictory. A perfectly faithful transcription of the letters would mystify many readers because, like other antebellum Americans, the authors of the Ellison letters did not consistently begin sentences with a capitalized word and end them with a period. To make the letters clear and legible to specialist and nonspecialist readers alike, we have altered the original text by capitalizing the first word in each sentence, by occasionally inserting commas, and by placing a period at the end. Because the letters often shift from one subject to another in a few brief sentences, we have attempted to keep this from becoming a source of confusion by introducing some paragraphing. In every other way, however, we have remained true to the original letters. We have retained the original order and spelling of words throughout, and we have not altered the original capitalization within sentences. When our reading of a word is not certain, we have enclosed the word in brackets. On the few occasions when we have exercised our editorial prerogative to clarify a passage by introducing a word, the word is enclosed in brackets and italicized.

In annotating the letters we have sought to supply all the information necessary to understand what a letter says, but not necessarily all that it means. The letters have many layers of meaning, more than we could hope to separate and explore in the notes. Instead, our goal is to give the reader enough information to understand the specific references in the letters and the context in which they are made. We have attempted to identify every individual, place, and event and to provide sufficient context to allow the reader to make an informed judgment about the significance of what is occurring. For each person we have tried to supply basic biographical information: age, occupation, wealth, and residence. In many cases one or more pieces of information are missing (and in a few cases, all of them), and we have therefore not been able to make all of the entries uniform. When a bit of information about a particular individual is not present, it is because, after exhausting every resource available to us, we could not find it.

In addition to identifying the specific references in the letters, we have also done all we can to uncover the relationships among the various persons mentioned. Only by discovering the crucial but nearly invisible network of relationships within the free mulatto community and between it and other free Negroes, slaves, and whites can the complex social history of the free brown aristocracy be understood. In antebellum Charleston spatial relationships were particularly important, and the reader can follow them on the city map that we have keyed to the references in the letters. Most of the landmarks mentioned in the letters more than a century ago are still standing. A visitor to Charleston today can see Grace Episcopal Church, St. Philip's and St. Michael's, Hibernian Hall and Mills House, the Battery and East Bay, as well as many of the residences of the white and brown aristocracies, including numbers 7 and 9 Coming Street, in which most of these letters were written. Yet the history of the city's free mulatto community is far less obvious and is encrusted by mythology and folklore. For example, as we investigated the documentary evidence for stories we heard or read, we discovered two persons who had been conflated by rumor into one, a "white" woman who was in fact of mixed ancestry, and a "Canadian" who was actually born and reared in Charleston. To separate truth from fiction and to piece together information on relationships, we have had to consult a wide variety of sources and, although we have done everything we could to avoid it, we have undoubtedly made some mistakes. We have chosen, therefore, to leave very clear tracks, to note the sources of our information specifically enough that any interested reader can follow our trail through the records.

Our decision to identify every reference, to establish wherever possible the relationships between individuals, and to provide enough contextual information to make the action intelligible means that many of the letters require more, sometimes far more, notation than the text of the letter itself. While this makes it necessary to do a good deal of page-turning to read the texts of certain letters with their associated notes, we hope the information in the notes will repay the effort.

Finally, in arranging the letters we have simply let them stand in chronological order as they probably were when the Leffelman girls first found them and as they certainly were when the Ellisons first read them. Although scattered across sixteen years, the letters convey a remarkably coherent account of the lives of the Ellisons and their Charleston friends. They are not an epistolary novel, but they can almost be read as one. We have chosen, therefore, to confine our editorial intervention to the notes, to give the letters no further introduction. We hope this allows readers to share the discovery of the letters' story. Prompted by the notes, the letters can speak for themselves.

NOTES

1. Interview with Mrs. Gery Leffelman Ballou and her mother, Mrs. Pauline Leffelman, May 29, 1981.

2. For a full discussion of the history of the Ellison family and the other issues introduced here, see the editors' *Black Masters: A Free Family of Color in the Old South* (New York and London, 1984). For fascinating accounts of wealthy free people of color in Louisiana, see Mills, *The Forgotten People* and Whitten, *Andrew Durnford*. The early life of a prosperous Virginian is recounted in Gatewood, ed., *Free Man of Color*.

3. This house was the girlhood home of Governor Miller's eldest daughter, Mary Boykin Miller Chesnut, whose famous Civil War memoir mentions her residence there. Woodward, ed., *Mary Chesnut's Civil War*, 411, 463–65.

4. A sizable number of family letters of a free Negro barber in antebellum Natchez are in the William Johnson Papers, Department of Archives, Louisiana State University, Baton Rouge. Other valuable collections of antebellum correspondence include the Madden Family Papers, University of Virginia Library, Charlottesville, and the Rapier Family Papers, Howard University Library, Washington, D.C. Letters written by free Negro emigrants to Liberia and directed mostly to white sponsors, friends, or former owners are assembled in Wiley, ed., *Slaves No More*. Letters written by both northern and southern free Negroes, many of them published in the contemporary antislavery press during the antebellum period, are collected in Woodson, ed., *The Mind of the Negro*. The closest

counterpart to the Ellison letters is the extensive diary of William Johnson covering the years 1835 to 1851, Hogan and Davis, eds., *William Johnson's Natchez*. For a biography of Johnson, see Davis and Hogan, *The Barber of Natchez*.

5. The term "free person of color" was a contemporary expression used by free Negroes and whites alike to refer to free persons of Afro-American descent. (Sometimes it also referred to descendants of American Indians.) We have adopted this common usage and employed the term interchangeably with "free Negro" and "free Afro-American" throughout this book. We have also adopted three other contemporary terms, "mulatto," "colored," and "brown." These words have acquired pejorative overtones and are not commonly used today. We have employed them in a nonpejorative sense, as the Ellisons and their friends did, to refer to individuals of mixed white and black ancestry. We have used the term "black" to refer to individuals of unmixed Afro-American descent. Both whites and Negroes were sensitive to the gradations of color, especially to the distinction between brown and black. Although we cannot always be certain of ancestry, we have tried to be consistent in applying the terms "brown" and "black."

6. Other items among the William Ellison papers are two slave passes from 1845, a receipt from 1847, a brief note of 1854 regarding an order for some blacksmith work, an 1858 receipt from a hardware store in Charleston, Henry Ellison's account with his Charleston factor for 1858 and 1860, an 1866 letter from a Charleston hardware dealer regarding an order the Ellisons had placed, two undated one-sentence notes to William Ellison inquiring about cotton gins, an unsigned fragment of a virtually indecipherable letter evidently dated October 1860, an undated fragment of a description of some agricultural machinery, and a postwar copybook from one of William Ellison's grandchildren. Ellison Family Papers, SCL.

7. For the best general history of southern free Negroes, see Berlin, *Slaves Without Masters*. A fine study of free Negroes in the North is Litwack, *North of Slavery*. A detailed examination of free Negroes in the nation's fifteen largest cities in 1850 is Curry, *The Free Black in Urban America, 1800–1850*. A revealing study of the political efforts of northern free Negroes in the antebellum period is Pease and Pease, *They Who Would Be Free*.

8. We have chosen to omit the three postwar letters. One, written by James D. Johnson, is undated, although it appears to

have been written in 1870. The other two, written by Henry Ellison in 1870, are a reply to Johnson's letter (apparently) that was never sent and a letter to a young family member in Charleston. Both are so badly faded that many sections are entirely illegible.

9. The best history of antebellum Charleston is Rogers, *Charleston in the Age of the Pinckneys*.

10. *Eighth Census*, 452. For a convenient set of population statistics for the entire South, see Berlin, *Slaves Without Masters*, 46–47, 136–37, 396–403.

11. *Eighth Census*, 452.

12. Although the published census did not report the numbers of mulattoes and blacks in the city (as opposed to the district, the surrounding countryside) of Charleston, the manuscript schedules of the 1860 census listed 721 free colored heads of household, of whom three-quarters were mulattoes.

13. The propertyless percentage is based on an analysis of the wealth reported by the 721 free Negro heads of household in the 1860 federal census. Of these individuals 16 percent owned one or more slaves and 17 percent owned $2,000 or more in real estate, according to the municipal tax assessments reported in *List of the Taxpayers of Charleston, 1860*, 315–34.

14. Ibid.

15. Owners of one or more slaves numbered 122; 117 owned real estate worth $2,000 or more. Ibid.

16. James M. Johnson to Henry Ellison, December 23, 1859, Ellison Family Papers.

17. James M. Johnson to Henry Ellison, December 23, 1860, ibid.

18. James M. Johnson to Henry Ellison, December 19, 1860, ibid.

19. James M. Johnson to Henry Ellison, August 28, 1860, ibid.

20. For an informative history of free Negroes in South Carolina, see Wikramanayake, *A World in Shadow*. Also useful is Henry, *The Police Control of the Slave*.

21. David Potter introduced the concept of personalism in a penetrating analysis of the agrarian theme in writings on the South. Although he never fully developed his insight, he implied that personalism was rooted deeply in southern life. He wrote:

On the face of it, it seems a matter of observation and not of theory to say that the culture of the folk survived in the South long after it succumbed to the onslaught of urban-industrial culture elsewhere. It was an aspect of this culture that the relation between the land and the people remained more direct and more primal in the South than in other parts of the country. (This may be more true for the Negroes than for the whites, but then there is also a question whether the Negroes may not have embodied the distinctive qualities of the Southern character even more than the whites.) Even in the most exploitative economic situations, this culture retained a personalism in the relations of man to man which the industrial culture lacks. . . . In the folk culture of the South, it may be that the relation of people to one another imparted a distinctive texture as well as a distinctive tempo to their lives. . . . This folk culture, we know, was far from being ideal or utopian, and was in fact full of inequality and wrong. . . ."

The South and the Sectional Conflict, 15–16.

22. Charleston *Courier*, December 16, 1859.

23. Michael J. Eggart, Annual Address, June 11, 1848, Minutes of the Friendly Moralist Society, 1841–1856, Special Collections, RSSL. For an analysis of this topic, see the editors' "'A Middle Ground.'" For a brief interpretive history of mulattoes in the United States, see Williamson, *New People*.

24. Degler, *Neither Black Nor White*.

25. Holt, *Black Over White*.

Letters

Key to Map of Charleston

1. Jeanette Bonneau
2. City Hall
3. Court House
4. John DeLarge
5. Joseph Dereef
6. Richard E. Dereef
7. James Eason
8. Eason's Foundry
9. Grace Episcopal Church
10. Hibernian Hall
11. Richard Holloway
12. Robert Houston
13. Institute Hall
14. James D. Johnson
15. Johnson's Tailor Shop

16. Benjamin K. Kinloch
17. Charles Macbeth
18. William McKinlay
19. Christopher G. Memminger
20. Mills House
21. Henry T. Peake
22. John Schnierle
23. St. Michael's Episcopal Church
24. St. Philip's Episcopal Church
25. Thomas L. Webb
26. Anthony Weston
27. Furman Weston
28. Jacob Weston
29. Samuel Weston
30. Westons' Tailor Shop

Charleston, 1860
From a map by A. H. Colton & Co. in Means and Turnbull, The Charleston
Directory. *Adapted by Karin Christensen.*

Charleston, S.C. Octr. 12th,
1848

To Messrs H. & R. Ellison,

Dear Friends, I have just taken up my Pen to inform you that the property of the Estate of T. S. Bonneau, Esq.,[1] is to be sold on next Thursday (Octr 19th inst) by the Master in Chancery providing there is no farther postponement by parties as the time has been entirely [*determined*] by appointment of Mr. E. Laurens[2] without consultation of Heirs, Executors, or any body else so far as I have been able to learn. We are about pursuing the course that I mentioned to you when you was in Town but which you did not say whether you would agree to or not, that is, to procure a Bidder to run the Property to what we consider to be a fair price as we find we have an under current to stem which, if we do not keep our eyes open, will sweep us away. I like to have your views, both of you, as to our plan of operations. As you know, there is some little risk of some of the property being knocked down to us. We will endeavor to avoid it if possible, but should it happen we can always sell again at Private sale, if all of the Heirs concur on one method. I think yet from what I have learnt that we may perhaps be able to get the value or nearly for the property tho one of our principle bidders has left the Feild and bought elsewhere. If you can get a Letter to me Wednesday Afternoon or even Thursday morning with your determination on the subject, I will be glad.

I have not seen an opportunity of sending the pepper as yet for Reuben. My love to all of the family. William[3] and his have arrived safe tho I have not seen them as yet.

We had a tremendous storm here Friday (11th) which blow'd down all of our Fence from the Gate spang to the Corner. Old Kinloch[4] & Ben was as pleased as Punch over it. The Old man was here by times this morning with John Holloway,[5] lest I might have undertaken the job myself.

All here joins me in love to all. Half past 11 o'clock. Good night.

J F W[6]

To Henry Ellison   Stateburg, S.C.

---

1. Thomas S. Bonneau directed a private school for free colored children in Charleston from about 1803 until his death in 1831. A leading member of the free colored community, he was admitted to the Brown Fellowship Society in 1816 and was very active in the aristocratic congregation of St. Philip's Protestant Episcopal Church. Shortly before his

death he owned six houses in Charleston and a number of slaves, some of whom he kept in the city and others on a plantation in the country.

According to a descendant who was an informant of the sociologist and historian E. Horace Fitchett, Bonneau's father was a French Huguenot colonist who settled at Port Royal in the eighteenth century, and his mother was a Seminole Indian. About 1805, Bonneau married Jeanette (or Jennette) Stephens, who was said to be of Scotch, Irish, and Indian parentage. They had nine children, two sons and seven daughters. Two of the daughters married Ellisons. Mary Elizabeth Bonneau married Henry Ellison and Harriett A. Bonneau married Reuben. The marriages must not have occurred before 1844 because in that year both Mary and Harriett were still listed as Bonneaus in the Charleston free Negro tax book.

The purpose of this letter was to consult Henry and Reuben as men interested in the Bonneau estate. The letter was written by the husband of another Bonneau daughter (see note 6, below). Bonneau's will provided that his property in town not be sold until his youngest child, Frances Pinckney Bonneau, reached the age of twenty. That provision had evidently been fulfilled; the sale men-

tioned in this letter was scheduled because Bonneau's son, Thomas C. Bonneau, filed suit against the executors of the will for the division of the estate. According to the advertisement that appeared in the Charleston *Courier* for five days preceding the sale, the property consisted of six town lots and the buildings on them, plus four slaves— a ten-year-old girl named Sally and an older woman named Fanny and her two sons, Isaac and Thomas. Buyers had to pay cash. Evidence in subsequent letters suggests that William Ellison purchased Isaac. See letters of December 28, 1858, note 1; February 25, 1860, note 1; and December 23, 1860, notes 1 and 2, below. Will of Thomas S. Bonneau, *Record of Wills*, Volume 39, 905– 907, CCL; Parish Register, St. Philip's Protestant Episcopal Church, 1810–1857, SCL; "List of Persons Admitted Members of the Brown Fellowship Society," *Rules and Regulations of the Brown Fellowship Society*, 25–27; Ellison family graveyard, Stateburg; Charleston Free Negro Tax Book, 1844, SCDAH; Fitchett, "The Free Negro in Charleston," 48, 93, 162, 193–95; Birnie, "The Education of the Negro in Charleston," 13–21; Charleston *Courier*, October 14, 16–19, 1848.

2. Edward R. Laurens was

master in chancery during the 1840s. Fay, *Charleston Directory*, and subsequent directories.

3. Presumably William Ellison, Jr., the brother of Henry and Reuben. About 1844 William also married a young woman from Charleston, Mary Thomson Mishaw, the daughter of John Mishaw, a member of the Brown Fellowship Society and a well-known boot- and shoemaker. Same sources as note 1.

4. The Kinlochs were a prominent free mulatto family in the city. The letter may refer to Richmond Kinloch, a millwright, a member of the Brown Fellowship Society and one of the executors of the will of Thomas S. Bonneau. Benjamin Kinloch was also a member of the Brown Fellowship Society. Same sources as note 1.

5. John Mitchell Holloway was a son of Richard Holloway (1776–1845), who was a member of the Brown Fellowship Society, a well-known carpenter in the city, and an exhorter in the Methodist Episcopal church. Thomas Bonneau's school met on Holloway's property on Beaufain Street. Holloway Scrapbook, 1811–1964, RSSL.

6. John Furman (also Fayman or Faman) Weston was a free mulatto machinist who married Louise (or Louisa) Potter Bonneau, a daughter of Thomas S. Bonneau, according to Fitchett, "Free Negro in Charleston," 48; Charleston Free Negro Tax Book, 1849, 1850, 1851, SCDAH.

Charleston, So Ca, Feb. 14,
1852

My Dear Minney,[1]

I received your affectionate letter and was quite glad to hear that you has recovered quite. We are all well except bad colds. Thank God. I am quite please with my little charge and I think if God [spares] my life & hers will be quite serviceable. I have begun with [hook] and needle already, though she knows nothing yet. But I hope in time will be quite smart. Sister [*illegible word*] is very active and smart at any thing. And she also is [*illegible word*] please with hers.

Do Tell Mr Miller[2] that there shall be nothing left undone for the improvement of his children, and if we are spared, please God, will never rue the day that he sent them to charleston. Tell Old Mrs. Benanhaly[3] [*illegible word*] I will [write] soon and whenever I pay Stateburgh a visit I will bring Jany[4] to see her. The children wanted to send something for Granny[5] but was not able this time, but next time will certainly do so. I remain your affectionation Sister

Frances[6]

Mrs M Ellison   Stateburgh

1. Mary Elizabeth (Bonneau) Ellison, the wife of Henry Ellison. See letter of October 12, 1846, note 1, above.

2. A. Miller, a forty-year-old free mulatto gin maker, was listed in the Ellison family compound in the 1850 federal census. He probably worked in William Ellison's gin shop. 1850 Population Schedules, Sumter, dwelling 1225, SCDAH.

3. Probably Elizabeth Benanhaly (Benenhaly), an elderly member of a group of people in Sumter District who were called and who called themselves "Turks." Tradition has it that the Benanhalys came to South Carolina from the Mediterranean, from Turkey or perhaps Morocco, and were Arabs. But the historian of Sumter County, Anne King Gregorie, admitted that she had "never seen any documentary material on the origins of the 'Turks'" and had "never solved" the "mystery." The Turks comprised several families. The Benanhalys and Scotts evidently arrived in Sumter District at the end of the eighteenth century at the invitation of General Thomas Sumter, the largest landholder in the area. The original community was augmented in the early nineteenth century by other families, including the Oxendines. This unusual surname was common among the group that became

the Lumbee Indians of North Carolina, suggesting perhaps a common origin. White society usually regarded the Turks as free people of color. Although the Turks were generally clannish, the Benanhalys were friends of the Ellisons. Eventually, two of the grandchildren of William Ellison, Sr., married members of the Oxendine and Benanhaly families. 1850 Population Schedules, Sumter, dwelling 1350, SCDAH; Anne King Gregorie to Ellen Perry, January 20, 1943 and Anne King Gregorie to Edward T. Price, September 20, 1950, Anne King Gregorie Papers, SCHS; Gregorie, *History of Sumter County*, 467–70; Berry, *Almost White*, 35–39, 186–90; Evans, *To Die Game*, 23–28, 51, 236.

4. It has been impossible to identify Jany with certainty, but it appears from the context of this letter and that of March 23, 1864, below, that she was probably the daughter of Frances P. (Bonneau) Holloway, and thus the niece of Mary Elizabeth (Bonneau) Ellison.

5. Perhaps Jeanette (Mrs. Thomas S.) Bonneau, the mother of Mary Elizabeth (Bonneau) Ellison and Frances Pinckney (Bonneau) Holloway, was visiting the Ellisons in Stateburg. Her granddaughter, Matilda Ellison, the five-year-old daughter of Henry and Mary E. Ellison, was ill and required visits from the doctor on February 16, 1852, and subsequent nights. "Granny" certainly did not refer to Mary E. Ellison's mother-in-law, Matilda Ellison (the wife of William Ellison, Sr.); she died January 14, 1850. Account Book of Dr. W. W. Anderson, 1844–1852, The Borough House Papers, SHC; Ellison family graveyard, Stateburg.

6. Frances Pinckney (Bonneau) Holloway ran a private school for free colored children on Coming Street in Charleston. According to an informant of E. Horace Fitchett, Frances married the free mulatto Richard Holloway, Jr., who—like his father—was a carpenter. Birnie, "Education of the Negro in Charleston," 19, 21; Fitchett, "Free Negro in Charleston," 48.

Charleston, June 25th, [*18*]55

Mr. Henry Elison,
Dear Sir,

Both of your letters came to hand safely, together with the money in one of them and that just in time. I shall pass it over to Mrs. Bonneau[1] to be appropriate to the purpose for which it was designed.

I hope that you and yours are in the enjoyment of that inestimable blessing health. Thank God myself and family are well. Give my love and respects to the family jointly.

Your obedient sert,
J Weston[2]

1. Henry Ellison's mother-in-law, Jeanette (Mrs. Thomas S.) Bonneau. In 1860 Mrs. Bonneau paid city taxes on one slave and real estate valued at $1,000. *List of the Taxpayers of Charleston, 1860*, 316.

2. Jacob Weston, a Charleston tailor and member of one of the most prominent free colored families in the city, belonged to the Brown Fellowship Society. In 1860 Weston paid municipal taxes on two slaves and real estate worth $11,600. Like Henry Ellison, Weston married one of the daughters of Thomas Bonneau, Sarah Ann (Bonneau) Weston, who died in 1848. Weston lived on Coming Street, next door to Mrs. Bonneau. Fitchett, "The Free Negro in Charleston," 48; 1850 Population Schedules, Charleston, Ward 4, dwelling 1067, SCDAH; Parish Register, Grace Episcopal Church, Charleston; Ford, *Census of Charleston, 1861*, 71; *List of the Taxpayers of Charleston, 1860*, 332; Charleston Free Negro Tax Book, 1848, SCDAH; Will of Jacob Weston, Charleston County Courthouse.

Stateburg, March 26th, 1857

Dear Henry,

Your letter of 23d instant was duly received and I perceived by it that you had not received mine of the 22d. John[1] went over the river yesterday. He saw Mr Ledinham.[2] He said that he had not sold but half of his crop of cotton and had not the money but when he got the money and was working on this side of the river that he would send his son with it and take up his account. He also saw Mr Van Buren[3] and he was ready to pay but before he did so he wished his overseer to certify to it. But John could not find him and, as it became late, he had to leave for home, but left the account with Mrs Mitchel, his wife. You will find inclosed Mrs Mathew Singleton[4] account. She will be found at No 4 Akins range.[5] Mr Turner[6] said that it was his fault that the account was not paid before. He thinks that she will get another gin. There is one of the saws in the new gin that is worn half in too.[7] He says that he will send the gin over to be repair and also another old gin, providing Mrs Singleton dont get a new gin.

As you did not get my letter in due time and for fear that you may not as yet received it, I will mention a few items of importance that I attended to. At once, if you have not done so, leave three hundred dollars in Messers Adams and Frost[8] hands, subject to my order, and also the money that I have borrowed from William.[9] Mr Benbow[10] wrote to me and I sent you a copy in the letter that I wrote you. Mr E Murray's[11] accounts and order was presented to him last Friday and he was to send his note when he sent to the post office, but he failed to do so.

I want you to get me a half doz. weeding hoes, No. 2; get two hand saws from Mr Adger[12] for the shop. I want you to get me 8 bags of guano. The above articles and instructions was stated in the other letter. I mention the same in case you should not have received my other letter. We are all well as usual. Give my respects to all my friends.

Your Father
William Ellison

Stateburg, March 26

Dear Henry,

As I have repeted the instruction in fathers letter of 22nd, it is nessessary that I [s]hould repeat the same in mine of 22d. I wish you to draw the amount of three hundred dollars that you will see in W. J. Elison Saving Bank Book with all the dividends and surplus dividends that it have drawn since deposited. Place it with the money that I gave you and my cotton money in the hands of Messers Adams an Frost subject to Fathers order. Reserve enough to pay for whatever expences you incur for me. Get Charles[13] to make a pair of drabatee pants[14] for John Buckner and pay him out of my money. I believe he is about to be married soon and he ask me for a present.[15] I dont wish the pants to exceed 5 or 6 dollars. Get a hankerchief for Charlotte,[16] one dollars worth of starch, 4 lbs of bird shot about this size ●. Gabriel[17] request me to say to you that the guatters that he spoke to you for is for his wife. No. 7's lether booties is what he want.

Our hands is imployed. Give my respects to Mrs Bonneau,[18] Mrs Weston,[19] Mr J D[20] & C J Johnson and families, James Lege[21] & Sister, and all my inquiring Friends. No more at present, but remain your affectionate Brother.

Mr Henry Ellison

William Ellison, Jr
Charleston, S C

1. John Wilson Buckner was the grandson of William Ellison, Sr. Buckner worked for his grandfather as a gin maker and, as is obvious from this letter, as a bill collector. Buckner was born January 23, 1831, to William Ellison's daughter Eliza Ann, who had married Willis Buckner on May 13, 1830, in the Church of the Holy Cross in Stateburg. 1850 Population Schedules, Sumter, dwelling 1225, SCDAH; "Children of William Ellison, July 25, 1838," Sumter County Records, Deeds of Conveyance, 1835–38, Book K, number 67, SCDAH; Record of the Claremont Parish, 1809–1866, Church of the Holy Cross, Stateburg, SCHS.

2. There were many Ledinhams, all of them white people, living in Richland District, west of the Wateree River. The Wateree was about four miles west

of the Ellisons' gin business in Stateburg.

3. While no Van Burens appear in the 1850 censuses for Richland or Sumter Districts, Angelica Singleton, daughter of Sumter planter Richard Singleton, married in 1839 Abram Van Buren, son of President Martin Van Buren. The couple resided in the North. Parler, *The Past Blows Away*, 21.

4. Perhaps Mrs. M. J. Singleton, the thirty-one-year-old wife of a white Sumter planter, but certainly a member of the large Singleton clan of white planters in Sumter with whom Ellison did extensive business. 1850 Population Schedules, Sumter, dwelling 1190, SCDAH; Singleton Family Papers, SHC.

5. Aiken's Street ran north from Columbus Street to Line Street in the northeast corner of the outskirts of Charleston.

Ford, *Census of Charleston, 1861*, 23.

6. Perhaps Arthur Turner, a fifty-year-old white farmer with no real estate but with a wife and nine children. Turner was apparently employed as Mrs. Singleton's overseer or plantation manager. 1850 Population Schedules, Sumter, dwelling 677, SCDAH.

7. The cotton gins that William Ellison manufactured contained circular saw blades—forged and sharpened in his shop—which separated the cotton fibers from the seeds. Ellison would custom build a gin with as many saws as a planter specified. Ellison advertised his gins in Sumter newspapers from the 1830s through 1860. No reference was made to his race; the advertisements were indistinguishable from those of other advertisers. Ellison's advertisement from the late 1840s read:

> Improved Cotton Gins
> Thankful for past favors, the subscriber wishes to inform the public, that he still *Manufactures Cotton Gins* at his establishment in *Stateburg* on the most improved and approved plan, of the most simple construction, of the finest finish, and of the best materials, to-wit: *Steel Saws and steel plated Ribs, case hardened*, in which he will sell for Two Dollars per Saw. He also

repairs old Gins and puts them in complete order, at the shortest notice. All orders for Gins will be promptly and punctually attended to.
> William Ellison
> Stateburg

In the 1850s Ellison added to his advertisement that "he thinks that the cotton ginned on one of those gins of the late improvement is worth at least a quarter of a cent more than the cotton ginned on an ordinary gin." Ellison's standard price remained two dollars per saw through 1860. For typical advertisements, see Sumter *Southern Whig*, June 2, 1831; Sumter *Banner*, December 13, 1848, and April 23, 1851, SCL.

8. E. L. Adams and E. H. Frost were white commission merchants and factors in Charleston, with offices on Adger's North wharf. They were the Ellisons' factors for many years. In 1860 they paid city taxes on over $31,000 in commissions on their factoring business, and each of the men was among the wealthier taxpayers in the city. Adams paid taxes on 12 slaves and real estate worth $25,000 in 1860; Frost also was taxed for 12 slaves and his real estate was valued at $23,000. Ferslew, *Directory of Charleston, 1860*; *List of Taxpayers of Charleston, 1860*, 1, 98.

9. William Ellison, Jr.

10. Probably either James H. Benbow, a forty-year-old white carpenter in Sumter District or Yabetha Benbow, a white farmer in Sumter who was about seventy-eight years old. 1850 Population Schedules, Sumter, dwelling 52, and 1860 Population Schedules, Sumter, dwelling 421, SCDAH.

11. Perhaps Edward L. Murray, who was a young white planter in Sumter District. There were several other white planters named Murray in the neighborhood. 1860 Population Schedules, Sumter, dwelling 1026, SCDAH.

12. Joseph Ellison Adger owned a hardware store on East Bay in Charleston, near the wharves owned by his father James Adger and, after 1858, by his brother James Adger, Jr. The Adgers, of course, were white. J. E. Adger's middle name came from his mother's side of the family. She was Sarah Elizabeth Ellison, the sister of white William Ellison, the Fairfield District planter who until 1816 owned as a slave William Ellison, Sr., free man of color. In 1860 J. E. Adger's hardware business was taxed for an inventory worth $65,200 and Adger himself was taxed for four slaves and real estate worth $12,000. Adger, *My Life and Times*, 21, 33, 36, 41; Ferslew, *Directory of Charleston, 1860*,

33; *List of Taxpayers of Charleston, 1860, 5.*

13. Charles J. Johnson, often referred to as Charley, was a free mulatto tailor in the shop of his father, James D. Johnson, a well-known tailor in Charleston. Charles's brother, James Marsh Johnson, was married to Eliza Ann, the sister of William Ellison, Jr. 1850 Population Schedules, Charleston, Ward 4, dwelling 414, SCDAH; Record of the Claremont Parish, 1809–1866, Church of the Holy Cross, Stateburg, SCHS.

14. Drabbet is a coarse linen fabric.

15. On April 8, 1857 John Buckner married a free woman of color named Jane. Evidence in subsequent letters suggests that Jane was the sister of James M. Johnson, John Buckner's stepfather. See letters of September 7, 1860, note 1, and September 16, 1860, note 5, below. Record of the Claremont Parish, 1809–1866, Church of the Holy Cross, Stateburg, SCHS.

16. Charlotte was listed as a slave in the inventory of the estate of William Ellison, Sr., made following his death in December 1861. Appraisement Bill, December 21, 1861, William Ellison Estate Papers, Box 151, Package 8, SCDAH.

17. Gabriel was another slave belonging to William Ellison,

Sr. Same source as above.

18. Jeanette (Mrs. Thomas
S.) Bonneau. She is referred to
throughout the letters as "Mrs.
Bonneau" or "Mrs. B."

19. Mrs. Bonneau's daughter,
Louisa P. Weston, lived on
Henrietta Street, several blocks
northeast of her residence and
those of the Johnsons on Coming Street. Charleston Free Negro Tax Books, 1848–1857,
SCDAH; Ford, *Census of Charleston, 1861*, 102.

20. James D. Johnson and
his wife Delia lived at 7 Coming
Street. His son Charles J.
(C. J.) Johnson lived next door
at 9 Coming. Henry may well
have been staying with the

Johnsons during his visit to
Charleston. Charleston Free
Negro Tax Books, 1850, 1851,
1855, 1857, SCDAH.

21. James Lege (or Legge)
and his sister Margaret Ann
Legge were cousins of James
M. Johnson. At the time of this
letter Margaret Ann lived with
James D. Johnson and his wife
at 7 Coming. See letter of January 9, 1860, note 9, below.
Charleston Free Negro Tax
Book, 1857, SCDAH; Will of
Margaret Ann Dereef, July 20,
1893, Probate Court, Charleston County Courthouse. We are
indebted to Susan Bowler for a
copy of this will.

Sunday, 18th Apl 1858

Dear Sir,[1]

According to your request that I should drop you a line to Charleston, I comply, though in these uneventful times you can expect nothing in the shape of news from this quarter. I received a few lines from Reuben[2] day before yesterday, in which he said all were well. He wrote pressingly that I should immediately procure for him a pair of young Pigeons, as if it were an affair of great importance. But I thought it a mere whim of his & have not yet spared the time to indulge it.

I feel rather better than I have done for some weeks, but I assure you there is no visible improvement for I am as poor & scrawny as ever & beside feel a depression of spirits which I cannot account for. It may foretoken some great calamity for "Coming events cast their shadows before" sometimes.

Mr Roach[3] asked me yesterday very particularly when you would return. I could not tell & did not like to show any curiosity by enquiring why he wished to know.

I must fill at least half a sheet & having nothing better to say, take the liberty of asking you to bring me a cheap shawl or a mantilla, which will cost about $2. And beside shewing your taste in the selection, get it to suit my age &c. Of course I mean dont let it be red or yellow, but of some grase, becoming, or genteel appearance.

I have a secret to tell you but cant trust it to paper.

Please remember me kindly [*to*] Mrs. Bonneau & her family & to Mr Johnson[4] & his. I suppose Matilda[5] is delighted. Do kiss her for me & tell her not to be too much pleased with Charleston & averse to returning to old friends in Sumter.

Mrs Murrell[6] asks yóu to bring a paper of green glazed cabbage & one or two of Leek seed & she prefers them from Landreths seed store. She will give me the money to hand you. Mr McFarlane[7] died at Dr. S Burgesses[8] of disease of the heart. Mr Lenoir[9] is sinking daily. I hear Mr Bradley[10] returned to Florida last Wednesday. People who have plenty of money can do as they please while they have health. Yet all come into life & go out of it alike.

Your sincere friend
S. Benenhaly[11]

1. The letter was probably addressed to Henry Ellison, but it may have been addressed to the elder William Ellison.

2. Reuben Ellison.

3. Perhaps J. B. Roach, a young white clerk in the town of Sumterville. 1860 Population

Schedules, Sumter, SCDAH.

4. James D. Johnson.

5. Matilda Ellison, the only child of Henry Ellison and his wife Mary Elizabeth (Bonneau) Ellison, was about eleven years old in 1858. Her mother had died in 1852. Matilda ultimately married into the Benanhaly family. 1850 Population Schedules, Sumter, dwelling 1224, and 1860 Population Schedules, Sumter, dwelling 696, SCDAH; Ellison family graveyard, Stateburg; Henry Ellison Estate Papers, Sept. 26, 1883, Bundle 176, Package 35, Sumter County Estate Papers, SCDAH.

6. Louisa Murrell, an elderly white woman who was the granddaughter of General Thomas Sumter, was a neighbor of the Ellisons in Stateburg. 1850 Population Schedules, Sumter, dwelling 1207, SCDAH; McGill, *Narrative of Reminiscences*, 97–98.

7. While no McFarlane appears in the antebellum Sumter District censuses, two young white planters with the name McFarland (William and Alexander) appear in 1850. 1850

Population Schedules, Sumter, dwellings 1311, 1315, SCDAH.

8. Samuel M. Burgess was a young white physician who was a neighbor of the Benanhalys and the Ellisons. 1860 Population Schedules, Sumter, dwelling 944, SCDAH.

9. Isaac Lenoir was an elderly white planter who lived near the Benanhalys. 1850 Population Schedules, Sumter, dwelling 1308, SCDAH.

10. Several white planters named Bradley lived near the Benanhalys and the Ellisons. 1850 Population Schedules, Sumter, dwellings 933, 1136, 1210, and 1860 Population Schedules, Sumter, dwellings 468, 1101, 1194, SCDAH.

11. Some thirty individuals with the name Benanhaly (or Benenhaly) appear in the 1860 census for Sumter District, but none has a given name beginning with the letter S. The name is also absent from the 1850 Sumter census. Still, S. Benanhaly was clearly a member of the community of Sumter "Turks." See letter of February 14, 1852, note 3, above.

Numbers 7 and 9 Coming Street in 1981
Photograph by Harold H. Norvell.

Charleston, Decr 28th, 1858

Friend Henry,

This will inform you that Isaac[1] has arrived safe bringing the shoes,[2] for which you have my thanks. He has reported himself to me and has conducted himself properly accordingly to request. I have obtained a ticket for him and will dispatch him tomorrow, Wednesday, according to appointment. His Parents begs to present thier thanks to you for permitting him to see them. The Old man has been working for me and requested me to write you to let him come. I intended to have done so, but your sending him has made it unnecessary.

We have received letters from all of our Canada folks.[3] They are all well and enjoying good health. In every letter they beg to be remembered to all of thier friends, especially those of Statesburg. Charles has been busy. He writes that it is quite cold and the air is very bracing. He has never enjoyed better health although he is sewing.

We are quite unwell at present although not laid up since the 21st inst but hope soon to be better. Give my respects to your father and the rest of the family and accept my dear friend my best regards for yourself.

J D Johnson[4]

1. Isaac was a slave of William Ellison, Sr. Evidently Ellison purchased him from the estate of Thomas S. Bonneau. See letter of October 12, 1848, note 1, above. Appraisement Bill, December 21, 1861, William Ellison Estate Papers, Box 151, Package 8, SCDAH.

2. The shoes may have been made in Stateburg by "Ellison & Johnson," apparently a joint enterprise of James M. Johnson and William Ellison. For examples of bills from "Johnson & Ellison" for "fine shoes" and "negro shoes," see the Moody Family Papers, SCL.

3. Charles Johnson, the son of James D. Johnson, had re-

cently moved to Toronto, Canada, with his wife, Gabriella (Miller) Johnson, and his daughter from a previous marriage, Charlotte. Other relatives of Johnson may also have been in Canada. The "Canada folks" figure in numerous subsequent letters. Canada West Census, 1861 (microfilm), Toronto, St. John's Ward, District 3, Reel 178, folio 598, PA.

4. James D. Johnson's son, James M. Johnson, was married to Henry's sister Eliza Ann and lived in the Ellison family compound in Stateburg. See letter of November 22, 1859, note 10, below.

Charleston, Novr 22/59

Dear Henry,

Yours of 20th inst is rec'd. I regret that misapprehension on my part has been the cause of trouble to you. Mrs G J[1] says she was relating to me what Charley had said to Wm & he then spoke in reference to the favorable chance her visit would afford to fill your order & forward the Clothes by her. Had you sent by Wm, the error was so glaring that I can only attribute my not noticing it before writing you to the confused state of my mind at the time. I will, however, endeavor to repair it by forwarding your order with the conditions annexed. Mrs. G. J. wrote twice since & 2 Letters has been recd from him. He[2] continues busy, has made some collections enabling him to pay off Journeymen, &c., & recd additional help from collection to the amt of ($20) Twenty Dolls made here.

With regard to the material aid, it was only a suggestion of mine based on the Tenor of his remarks, a synopsis of which I gave, knowing that you felt a lively interest in his[3] welfare & having the assurance that his regard for you as a *"Tried Friend"* is unabated. And as your Father was anxious for me to give information when I did not possess it, I deemd it proper that he[4] should be advised now that the facts were before me & if, entertaining (as I believe he does) the best wishes for his[5] prosperity, he[6] saw fit to assist him[7] pecuniarily, altho unauthorized to do so, I am confident it would be cordially accepted &, if necessary, would guarantee to protect him from loss in the premises. Further this respondent saith not.

I am glad to hear that the Baby[8] is better. All joins me in Love to All at both halls.[9]

I [sent Mr G. L. bookes.]

Thine Ever
J M Johnson[10]

1. Gabriella (Miller) Johnson, the wife of Charles (or Charley) Johnson, was living in Toronto but was on a visit to Charleston. The account of the mixup about the order is muddled. Apparently, William Ellison, Jr., was visiting Charley in Canada. Henry had placed an order for some clothing with Charley. Either Charley or William suggested that Gabriella bring the clothes with her on her visit to Charleston. The saga of clothing continues through several subsequent letters. State laws of 1822 and 1835 prohibited free persons of color from returning to South Carolina after they had left. This and numerous subsequent references in the letters make clear that the law was routinely ignored. In less than a year, that practice changed drastically.

2. Charles J. Johnson. He

was struggling to establish his tailoring business in Toronto. When the Canadian census was taken in January 1861, he reported a total capital of only $200. Canada West Census, 1861, Toronto, St. John's Ward, District 3, Reel 178, folio 598, PA.

3. Again, Charles J. Johnson.

4. Henry's father, William Ellison, Sr.

5. Charles J. Johnson.

6. William Ellison, Sr.

7. Charles J. Johnson.

8. Johnson may have been referring to his stepson John Buckner's baby daughter, Harriet Ann, who was born March 25, 1858. If so, the baby did get better since Harriet Ann was baptized in the Church of the Holy Cross in Stateburg on June 2, 1860, sponsored by James M. Johnson and his wife Eliza Ann. Record of the Claremont Parish, 1809–1866, Church of the Holy Cross, Stateburg, SCHS.

9. The Ellisons referred to the residences in their family compound as "halls." The home of William Ellison, Sr., was referred to as Wisdom Hall, and the residence next door where James M. Johnson and Eliza Ann (Ellison) Johnson lived was called Drayton Hall. The Johnsons' residence was jointly owned by William Ellison, Sr., and James Drayton Johnson. The use of these terms was apparently confined to the family. Aristocratic white families around Stateburg commonly gave their homes similar names, such as Edgehill, Woodfield, and Marden. Statement of the Estate of William Ellison for 1862, by Henry Ellison, Executor, William Ellison Estate Papers, Sumter County Estate Papers, Box 151, package 8, SCDAH; Sumter, *Dedicated to the Past*, 3, 8–10.

10. James M. Johnson, who sometimes signed his letters "J M J", had left his Stateburg home and returned to his native Charleston to help out in his father's tailor shop. Johnson had moved to Stateburg in 1842 and had lived there since then. He became a communicant in the Church of the Holy Cross in Stateburg in 1843 and married Eliza Ann (Ellison) Buckner in the church on February 26, 1845. Charleston Free Negro Tax Books, 1838–1842, SCDAH; Record of the Claremont Parish, 1809–1866, Church of the Holy Cross, Stateburg, SCHS.

Christopher G. Memminger
From an original in the South Carolina Historical Society. Photograph by
Harold H. Norvell.

Charleston, Decr 23d/59

Dear Henry,

I hope this will find you relieved from your cold. I am annoyed with one. The wedding came off in style. Nat Fuller[1] was the caterer. He had oysters served for E Ann[2] at 9 o'clock. We left soon after. We had two bottles of champagne broached before leaving & did not even eat a piece of cake. The crowd was a large & respectable one. Mr Gadsden[3] performed the ceremony, Dr Hanckel[4] being sick. There were 10 attending of each sex. Some of the bridesmaids left before we did for Savannah. Beard[5] went down with them but took care to get back before supper. The bride & groom are gone on a Tour in the country.

Matilda[6] was at Home today for the first time. She is well. Mrs Bonneau is quite feeble. R Kinloch[7] gets married shortly, also Miss Gourdin,[8] an apprentice of Mrs Lee.[9]

Do tender my congratulations to your Father on the adjournment of the Legislature. He ought to read Col Memminger's[10] speech against Moore's bill.[11] It is in the Courier of 16th. I prophesied from the onset that nothing would be done affecting our position.

We have sent some little nick nacks for the children, not having room for the grown folks. You must come down & follow the fashion. I heard a few days ago my cotton was sold, but did not learn the rates. I will be able to settle up with your Father for Bagging, Rope, &c. Do see that Sarah[12] behaves herself & salts the creatures regularly. We have not heard from Charley for some days. Father,[13] Mother, Gabriella, & E Ann unite with me in wishing you & all at Wisdom Hall a Merry Christmas. As ever, I am yrs truly

J M J

1. Nat Fuller was a free man of color whose catering business was well known in the city. In the recent mayoral election, when the activities of slaves and free persons of color had been the subject of heated discussion, a wedding at Zion Presbyterian Church similar to the one described in this letter prompted "A Slaveholder" to write the *Mercury*, "Well may we exclaim, 'where are we drifting to?' when in a slaveholding community the 'nuptials of *blacks*' are celebrated in a spacious temple of the Most High—where a bridal party of a score and ten in numbers are transported to the modern centre of fashion and false philanthropy in gay equipages— and where hundreds of others, robed in extravagant costumes, witness possibly with eyeglass in hand, this the dawn of a new

fashioned sentiment, and where harangues are delivered on 'rights'." Means and Turnbull, *The Charleston Directory [1859]*, 72; Charleston Free Negro Tax Book, 1862, CLS; Charleston *Mercury*, October 25, 27, 1859.

2. Eliza Ann (Ellison) Johnson, the wife of James M. Johnson.

3. Reverend Christopher P. Gadsden was rector of St. Luke's Protestant Episcopal Church in Charleston. Ferslew, *Directory of Charleston, 1860*, 31.

4. Reverend Christian Hanckel was the rector of St. Paul's Protestant Episcopal Church, which was located on Coming Street, at the corner of Vanderhorst, only a few blocks from James M. Johnson's father's home. The wedding referred to in the letter was probably at St. Paul's. Ibid.

5. Probably Samuel or Anthony Beard. Neither paid city property tax in 1860 or reported any wealth to the federal census marshal. The two brothers were among the tailors in the free colored community of Charleston and may well have worked for Johnson. 1860 Population Schedules, Charleston, Ward 8, dwelling 46, SCDAH.

6. Matilda Ellison, Henry's daughter.

7. Richmond Kinloch was a free mulatto carpenter about twenty years old. Although Kinloch did not pay municipal property taxes, in the federal census he reported owning real estate worth $3,000. 1860 Population Schedules, Charleston, Ward 4, dwelling 808, SCDAH.

8. Although Miss Gourdin cannot be positively identified, she was almost certainly a young free woman of color who worked as an apprentice mantua maker for Mrs. Lee.

9. Elizabeth Lee was a free woman of color about forty-two years old who worked as a mantua maker in her home at 9 Coming, which had been vacated by Charles Johnson's move to Canada. In 1860, according to the federal census, her daughter Charlotte and another relative named Agnes (possibly her sister-in-law) lived with her and worked as mantua makers. Neither Elizabeth Lee nor her husband, Edward S. Lee, paid any city property taxes in 1860 or reported any wealth to the federal census marshal. In the 1850 federal census, however, Edward Lee reported owning real estate valued at $4,000. In 1850 he worked as a hair dresser; in 1860 his occupational listing was "sexton." He was a member of the Brown Fellowship Society. 1850 Population Schedules, Charleston, Ward 1, dwell-

ing 216; 1860 Population
Schedules, Charleston, Ward 4,
dwelling 438, SCDAH; Means
and Turnbull, *Charleston Directory, 1859,* 121; Minutes of
the Brown Fellowship Society,
1869–1911, RSSL.

10. Christopher Gustavus
Memminger was a promi-
nent lawyer and politician in
Charleston and a member of the
Charleston delegation to the
South Carolina House of Representatives. Later he served as
the Secretary of the Treasury of
the Confederacy. Memminger
lived at the northwest corner of
Wentworth and Smith streets,
about three blocks from Johnson's house on Coming. He was
a parishioner of Grace Episcopal Church, two and a half
blocks east on Wentworth
Street, as were the Johnsons
and other well-established families in the free colored community. Memminger was a wealthy
man. In 1860 he paid city taxes
on real estate worth $18,000
and on eight slaves. His holdings outside the city were sizable, for he reported to the
federal census marshal real
property worth $25,000 and
personal property valued at
$150,000. *Dictionary of Ameri-
can Biography,* s.v. "Memminger, Christopher"; Ferslew,
Directory of Charleston, 1860,
101; Parish Register, Grace
Episcopal Church, Charleston;
Christopher Gustavus Mem-

minger Papers, (microfilm),
SHC; *List of the Taxpayers of
Charleston, 1860,* 182; 1860
Population Schedules, Charles-
ton, Ward 4, dwelling 731,
SCDAH.

11. Edward Moore was a
member of the South Carolina
House of Representatives from
York District in the upcountry.
Moore introduced a bill requiring all free Negroes in South
Carolina to be sold into slavery
on March 1, 1860; until then
they would be allowed to leave
the state. Moore argued that
"these trifling vagabonds should
be sold or compelled to leave
the state." During the three-
hour debate on Moore's bill and
two other proposals—one to enslave free persons of color convicted of certain crimes and
another to provide for the grad-
ual removal of all free people of
color—Memminger defended
free people of color and argued
against all three of the bills. According to the account of his
speech in the Charleston *Courier,* December 16, 1859, he
said: "The free negro is a subject, and in all countries where
the definition of subject is understood, he has his rights just
as well as any other citizen. The
citizen may vote, but the subject
and every man is entitled to the
protection of our laws. That
will be found to be the sound
policy of South Carolina. Was it
not through the instrumentality

of a free colored man that a for-
midable insurrection was discovered and quelled. Have we
not again and again voted testi-
monials to people of that class.
Within his district there were
men of most estimable character, and as a general rule, take
an equal number of them and
an equal number of those [white
men] who come nearest to
them, and there will be found
more amongst the latter who
are demoralizing our slaves. It
was not the policy of the State
to set those people who are our
friends against us." Moore's bill
was tabled and the Charleston
delegation supported Mem-
minger's motion for indefinite
postponement of the bill to enslave free blacks convicted of
certain crimes. But a majority
of the House opposed Mem-
minger's motion, and the latter
bill was sent to the Senate,
where it was bottled up in the
Committee on the Judiciary.
None of the more than twenty
bills proscribing free people of
color was approved by the legislature but all of them remained
in the hopper, ready to be called
up at the 1860 session. *Reports
and Resolutions of the General
Assembly*, 129, 148, 160–63,
179, 211; Charleston *Courier*,
December 15, 1859.

12. Sarah was a slave who
belonged to William Ellison,
Sr., but apparently served his
daughter, Eliza Ann (Ellison)
Johnson. Sarah was baptized in
the Church of the Holy Cross in
1850 and was bequeathed to
Eliza Ann for her "Sole and
separate use" in Ellison's will
written in 1851. A codicil of
May 1861 revoked the bequest
and provided that Sarah be sold
by his executors and the proceeds divided among his heirs.
No other slave was thus singled
out. The motivation for this
provision of the codicil is unknown; in some way or other
Sarah had evidently displeased
the elder Ellison. Will of William Ellison and Appraisement
Bill, December 21, 1861, William Ellison Estate Papers,
Sumter County Estate Papers,
Box 151, Package 8, SCDAH;
Records of the Claremont Parish, 1809–1866, Church of the
Holy Cross, Stateburg, SCHS.

13. James D. Johnson. His
wife (James M. Johnson's
mother) was Delia Johnson.
Charleston Free Negro Tax
Books, 1833–1844, SCDAH.

Jany 9th/60

Dear Henry,

Your favor of 1st inst was recd on 5th. We were glad to hear from you & as you made no complaints arrive at the pleasant conclusion that you are well again.

Business has taken a brush up since the Holidays, but Money is Scarce with us. A letter has been recd by Mrs. J[1] from Charley dated 22d, stating that your Clothes had been forwarded & a True Bill sent you. The Duty he said would have to be paid on arrival. I have been enquiring at the Express Office. It is not there so that I infer it must be sent Direct through to you. Do let us hear if recd &c., &c.

The Bride & groom has returned. E Ann has been to see her. She is very lively & with her brief experiences appears to be highly pleased. We continue to have disagreeable weather. Bishop Davis[2] is in the City. E Ann has been troubled with headache for a few days. I see D Burgess[3] who gave me information of D B Mowson[4] in Town. He married at Kingstree[5] recently. If you wish any further enquiry made & get word in time, I will do so. I hope I am & the children are better of their colds.

Say to J W B[6] I will settle Mr Norris[7] Bill when I come up. In the interim you can have Jas. Norris note disct & if he chooses to pay any thing, he can do so after having the amt due by Mr Jacobs[8] credited in my favor.

Father & Mother, Gabriella & Margaret[9] join with E Ann & Self in wishing you & all at Wisdom & Drayton Halls a Happy New Year &c.

Kinloch[10] goes off on Wednesday night.

I enclose Mr M's[11] remarks. I have pledged your Father as a Contributor to a present to be sent him. I was present when Mr Houston[12] Returned him thanks in behalf of our people. He recd it very cordially & throws the blame on the up country members.[13]

As ever yrs truly
J M Johnson

1. Gabriella Johnson, the wife of Charles J. (Charley) Johnson.

2. Thomas Frederick Davis had been the Episcopal Bishop of South Carolina since 1853. He had served as pastor of Grace Church in Camden since 1846 and was well known to Episcopalians throughout the state because he kept a strenuous schedule of visitations to the various parishes. In October 1855, for example, he had confirmed Abraham, one of William Ellison's slaves, in a ceremony at Holy Cross Church in Stateburg. Holy

Cross Episcopal Church Record, 1808–1863, Stateburg, SCHS; Thomas, *A Historical Account of the Protestant Episcopal Church in South Carolina*, 706–708.

3. It has not been possible to identify this individual. While there were many persons, both whites and Negroes, living in Sumter District with the name Burgess, none had the proper initial.

4. D. B. Mowson does not appear in the federal censuses for Sumter District.

5. Kingstree was a small town on the Black River, about 70 miles north of Charleston along the North Eastern Railroad.

6. John W. Buckner, James M. Johnson's stepson. See letter of March 26, 1857, note 1, above.

7. While there were many individuals with the name Norris in Sumter District, none, according to the federal censuses, had the first name James.

8. Perhaps Alexander Jacobs, a thirty-four-year-old free mulatto tailor in Sumter District. 1860 Population Schedules, Sumter, dwelling 134, SCDAH.

9. Margaret Ann Legge was James M. Johnson's cousin. She was living in James D. Johnson's home on Coming Street. In his 1867 will, the elder Johnson bequeathed to her the interest on his deposits in the Charleston Savings Bank. In 1869 she married Johnson's close friend, Richard E. Dereef. See letter of March 26, 1857, note 21, above. Will of James D. Johnson, July 13, 1867, James D. Johnson Estate Papers, Probate Court, Charleston County Courthouse; Charleston Free Negro Tax Book, 1857, SCDAH; 1870 Population Schedules, Charleston, Ward 4, dwelling 904, SCDAH.

10. Presumably Richmond Kinloch, whose impending marriage was mentioned in the letter of December 23, 1859. See note 7 of that letter, above.

11. C. G. Memminger. Presumably, the remarks were those printed in the *Courier*, December 16, 1859. See letter of December 23, 1859, note 11, above.

12. Robert Houston was one of the leaders in the free colored community in Charleston. He was a member of the Brown Fellowship Society and a well-known tailor, with a shop on King Street about three blocks north of James D. Johnson's shop. Like Memminger, he was an active member of Grace Episcopal Church. Although Houston was not one of the wealthier members of the free colored community, he did own a modest amount of property. In 1860 he paid municipal taxes on real estate valued at $2,000,

presumably his home and shop on King Street. 1860 Population Schedules, Charleston, Ward 5, dwelling 19, SCDAH; Ford, *Census of Charleston, 1861*, 123; Parish Register, Grace Episcopal Church, Charleston; *List of the Taxpayers of Charleston, 1860*, 324; Minutes of the Brown Fellowship Society, January 7, 1869–July 6, 1911, RSSL.

13. In the 1859 legislature, some of the strongest proponents of legislation restricting, expelling, or enslaving free people of color were from the upcountry. See letter of December 23, 1859, note 11, above.

Charleston, Jany 20th, 1860

Dear Henry,

Your respective favors are recd. I have been awaiting further news from the Box, but failing to do so I must proceed to answer your interrogatories.

As it regards the Cotton Seed, I expect to get more for them here than they would be worth to you. I told Mr Bowie[1] that I did not expect to plant when he settled with me for the Cotton. He thinks he can find a Market for them, & until they are sold I have the privilege of Storing them in his back store free of charges.

Matilda[2] dined with us the day after I recd your last. I sent the Bill you enclosed to Mrs F. P. Holloway[3] by her. She is well & says her Grandmother[4] is better than She was. You have my full consent to haul the leaves on the terms stated, provided your Father does not object.

I have made repeated enquiries after the Box & learn from the Agent that their Line, Adams,[5] does not extend beyond Albany & Boston northward. They do receive & transmit packages from Thompson's Express, which extends to Canada. But at this Season there are so many interruptions that they are unable to fix upon any time. They have no apprehensions for its safety & are confident as soon as it reaches Albany or Boston, their Terminus, it will be put through safe. So that you see nothing would be gained by telegraphing. Charley wrote that from a press of business he was quite unwell & this may be cause of his not writing or the letters may be retarded by the Ice. He wrote that the Bill would be recd within the Box. I find that their being no regular Agent at Claremont,[6] freight would have to be prepaid here if directed there. They have an Agent at Camden.[7] I got myself a Blk Raglan which is at your Service. It is capacious enough for you, but a little abused as I had to wear it in the week until I made a Tweed over Jacque that answers for present use.

E Ann expects to be returning shortly & requests that Sarah[8] would be made to clean out the Fowl House properly & bury the contents in the poultry lot adjoining. If I can be spared, I propose accompanying her & will attend to forwarding up anything you may wish procured here.

That was a very amusing piece you sent me. I enclose a strip relating to the Earthquake.[9] It was sensibly felt at our house; although unacquainted with the phenomena, I attributed the concusions to the shock of an Earthquake & while Mother[10] was calling to see what was under the House, Mrs Lee[11] sent to enquire if our House shook as theirs did, which confirmed my impression.

I saw Bynum Moore.[12] He thinking Col M.[13] will buy the colt. He invited me up to the course to see his Fillies. Winter[14] gave us a call; he has a Birth in Florida.

Bishop Paine[15] of Africa is here. He gives interesting accounts of his Mission. I heard him twice. On the last occasion he sung "There is a happy land" translated in the native dialect as sung by them. It was beautiful.

Mr Broughton[16] of Clarendon is here. We were invited to the wedding of Mr Hoff's[17] adopted daughter & Mr E F Baxter[18] at 5 A M Monday. They were to leave for Georgetown at 7 A M. Dr Marshall[19] married them at 6 o'clock at Mr Hoff's.

Father, Mother, E. Ann, Gabriella, & Margaret join me in love to all at Wisdom and Drayton Halls.

> As Ever Thine Ever
> J M Johnson

1. John A. Bowie was a commission merchant on Central Wharf in Charleston. James S. and Langdon Bowie were wholesale dry goods dealers on Meeting Street. All of them were white men. Johnson may have been settling his bill for cloth with the receipts from the sale of his cotton. Johnson probably did not have much cotton to sell. Most likely, he worked a small piece of William Ellison's plantation; he did not report owning any real or personal property in the federal censuses of 1850 or 1860, nor was he listed as a farm operator in the agricultural schedules. Ferslew, *Directory of Charleston, 1860*, 43; *List of the Taxpayers of Charleston, 1860*, 29.

2. Henry's daughter, Matilda Ellison.

3. In 1860 Frances Pinckney (Bonneau) Holloway—Henry Ellison's sister-in-law—was evidently living with her mother on Coming Street, where Matilda Ellison may well have been staying. Charleston Free Negro Tax Book, 1860, Carter G. Woodson Papers, (microfilm), Manuscript Division, LC. See letter of February 14, 1852, note 6, above.

4. Jeanette (Mrs. Thomas S.) Bonneau.

5. The Adams Express Company shipped freight in and out of Charleston.

6. Claremont was a stop on the South Carolina Railroad between Charleston and Camden. The depot was about two and a half miles from the Ellisons.

7. Camden was then a small town about twenty miles north of Stateburg. It was the home of Mary Boykin (Miller) Chesnut, who had spent her early years in the house now occupied by Wil-

liam Ellison. Ellison had purchased it in 1835 from her father, the former United States senator and governor of South Carolina, Stephen D. Miller. Sumter Conveyances, Book K, 64, SCDAH; Woodward, ed., *Mary Chesnut's Civil War*, 463–65.

8. Sarah was a slave who worked for Eliza Ann Johnson. See the letter of December 23, 1859, note 12, above.

9. An earthquake occurred about 7:00 P.M. January 19, 1860. It was felt in Charleston, Columbia, Sumter and elsewhere in the southeast. According to the Charleston newspapers, the quake did not cause serious damage. Charleston *Mercury*, January 20, 28, 1860; Charleston *Courier*, January 21, 1860.

10. Delia Johnson, James M. Johnson's mother.

11. Elizabeth Lee, the wife of Edward S. Lee. See letter of December 23, 1859, note 9, above.

12. Probably John B. Moore, who brought a stable of racehorses to Charleston for the annual Jockey Club races in February. Moore was a young, very wealthy white planter from the Stateburg area, which was a center of thoroughbred racing. Charleston *Mercury*, December 23, 1859, January 26 and February 1, 1860; Charleston *Cou-*

rier, January 20, 25, 1860; 1860 Population Schedules, Sumter, dwelling 1136, SCDAH; Singleton Family Papers, SHC.

13. Perhaps James S. Moore, a planter, or M. L. Moore, a physician, both of whom were wealthy white men who lived near John B. Moore. 1860 Population Schedules, Sumter, dwellings 1142, 1177, SCDAH.

14. Apparently, Winter was a stallion and Florida, a mare. The reference suggests that the horses were known to Henry Ellison and James M. Johnson.

15. Bishop John Payne, a white man, was an Episcopal missionary on the west coast of Africa. He was on a tour of parishes in the United States and was in Charleston from January 15 through 22. According to the *Southern Episcopalian*, the "colored members" of the Episcopal churches in Charleston supported a teacher in his mission on the Cavalla River. Something of Bishop Payne's perspective on his twenty-three years in Africa is revealed in his remarks at St. Mark's in Baltimore, where he referred "to that mysterious Providence which had brought so many millions of its natives to our shores, fused their several hundred different dialects into one language, and enlightened very many with the knowledge of the saving grace of Christ. . . ."

Southern Episcopalian, 6 (February, 1860), 595–97; 7 (August, 1860), 51.

16. Probably a white planter in Clarendon District, immediately south of Sumter District.

17. John Hoff (or Hoffe) was a free mulatto tailor in Charleston. He paid municipal taxes on real estate worth $2,400 and on one slave. His daughter Harriet was about eighteen years old in 1860 and worked as a dressmaker, probably helping her mother Ann, who was a seamstress. 1860 Population Schedules, Charleston, Ward 8, dwelling 216, and 1850 Population Schedules, Charleston Neck, dwelling 433, SCDAH; *List of the Taxpayers of Charleston, 1860*, 323.

18. Edward F. Baxter was a free mulatto carpenter about twenty-five years old. Baxter paid no city property taxes and, according to the federal census, owned no property. Baxter and his new bride were living in Hoff's household in June 1860 when the federal census was taken. 1850 Population Schedules, Charleston Neck, dwelling 523, and 1860 Population Schedules, Charleston, Ward 8, dwelling 216, SCDAH.

19. Reverend A. W. Marshall was rector of St. John's Protestant Episcopal Church, on Amherst Street at the corner of Hanover. Ferslew, *Directory of Charleston, 1860*, Appendix, 30.

January 24th, 1860

Dear Henry,

I hastily acknowledge the Receipt of yours of 22d. I cannot answer all your enquiries at this time, but assure you that we have left no means untried to try & facilitate some intelligence of the Box. Gabriella has written twice on the subject since she last heard & confidently hopes to hear this week. By reference to Monday's paper you will see that the mails just got through after a long detention.

I congratulate Wm[1] on his good luck & hope the same awaits us.

I saw Col M's[2] fillies since I wrote. They are fine & have the praise of being the best groomed horses in the country. Florida is here. She was beat by Fanny Park, an old mare of Mrs Bradford in Bynum's care.

You must excuse this & expect me with a verbal detail on Tuesday 31st. Please send to depot[3] for us. The Raglan[4] will be forthcoming also. E Ann & the Family join me in Love to all at Wisdom Hall.

Yrs Truly
James

1. Apparently William Ellison, Jr.

2. See the letter of January 20, 1860, notes 12, 13, and 14, above.

3. The train depot at Claremont.

4. Johnson was taking Henry the black raglan he had mentioned in the previous letter (January 20, 1860), to be used until the box of new clothes arrived that Henry had ordered from Charley.

Charleston, Feby 25th/60

Dear Henry,

I was glad to hear that Isaac[1] returnd & hope he has seen his folly.

With regard to the Clothes, in view of the Duty, Charlie authorised his wife to draw out a Bill to conform to it & destroy the one he sent, as he did not wish you to be taxed for your kind patronage. The Clothes were pronounced to be of capital material here by judges.[2] The style of trimming is not as extravagant there as here, as I found out by Mr Roberts english[3] clothes. The Over Coat is a superior Beaver Cloth which they tell me is better than that of Mr Frierson, of which I had a piece. Gabriella will Remit the money whenever you please to forward it.

Father & the Family join in their best Respects.

I saw Mr Brahe.[4] He says he sent the leather on Monday 13th. I enclose a slip for Wm. It is a late acct of a Fire in Brantford.[5] McLean & others burnt out, a loss of $150,000. The slip is mistaken. Do hand those copies of "American Republican"[6] in the Box to E. Ann.

Thine Ever
J M Johnson

H. Ellison, Esqr.

1. Isaac was a slave of William Ellison, Sr. See letter of December 18, 1858, note 1, above.

2. Apparently the box of clothes had arrived in Charleston while James M. Johnson was visiting his home in Stateburg. The Adams Express Company listed one box for W. M. Ellison in a list of unclaimed freight published in the Charleston *Courier*, February 13, 1860.

3. Robert English and the Mr. Frierson Johnson referred to were aristocratic white planters with estates near Stateburg. Means-English-Doby Papers, SCL.

4. A. H. Brahe, a white man, was an importer of leather with a shop at 13 Hayne in Charleston. The inventory was assessed at $6,000 for city taxes. The Ellisons used leather belting for their cotton gins, and "Ellison and Johnson" used leather in making shoes. See letter of December 28, 1858, note 2, above. Ferslew, *Directory of Charleston, 1860*, 38, 43; *List of the Taxpayers of Charleston, 1860*, 31.

5. The *Courier* reported (February 22, 1860) that a fire in Brantford, Canada West, broke out the morning of February 17 in the dry goods store of McLean and spread along two streets, destroying some twenty-three buildings. The report estimated the loss at be-

tween one and two hundred thousand dollars. Brantford contained a good many Negroes who were born in the United States, according to the Canada West Census, 1861 (microfilm), Brant County, Ontario, Reel 79, Genealogical Library, Church of Jesus Christ of Latter-day Saints, Salt Lake City, Utah.

6. Probably issues of the Baltimore newspaper formerly titled the *American Republican and Daily Clipper*, although its current title was *American and Commercial Advertiser*. Gregory, *American Newspapers, 1821–1936*, 258.

Charleston, April 24th, 1860

Dear Henry,

I will now Report progress. Mother[1] is at home again & we are as well as you left us. Miss M.[2] passed Saturday sporting a Hat & after a long promenade, took the omnibus by which means she got a Beaux who escorted her home afoot. He said he was willing to make apology, &c.

The Artillery[3] paraded in honor of opening of Savannah Road[4] & Grant[5] gave out. They were going to salute the Gov of N.Y.[6] & was missing until dark. In the meantime, Mr. Lacoste[7] came in & told us all about it. When Grant returned he said it was just so, they were saluting the Gov of N Y.

Sunday the Convention[8] was the theme of most of the Reports. The crowd still keeps thin & prices are Reduced. The [*two or three illegible words; torn page*] here yesterday & gave us a free ride. The Boston Band[9] also favord the public with Music. The Police passd here making arrests of suspicious & rowdy characters twice yesterday.[10] And if you have lost the Rights you ought to find solace in making a Retreat from the Heat.

I hope you have found all Right & may pursue your unvarying course uninterrupted by [advisers].

I send you the late papers with this. When you get through with the Evening News,[11] give it to E Ann. Father & the Family join me in Kind Regards. As ever I am

Yours sincerely
J M Johnson

1. Delia Johnson, James M. Johnson's mother.

2. Miss Mary M., as she is identified in the letter of May 5, 1860, was certainly a young free woman of color; several women with that name and initial were listed in the 1860 Free Negro Tax Book. Carter G. Woodson Papers, Manuscript Division, LC.

3. The Marion Artillery, a local militia unit, paraded to the railroad depot in Charleston and fired a thirteen-gun salute in honor of the first train to arrive from Savannah. Charleston *Mercury*, April 23, 1860.

4. The Charleston and Savannah Railroad was officially opened on Saturday, April 21, when a delegation from Charleston met another from Savannah at Grahamville, a midway point on the line. Charleston *Mercury*, April 23, 1860.

5. It appears from the context that Grant was a slave. According to the city tax book, James D. Johnson owned three

slaves in 1860; Grant may have been one of them. There were, however, several free men of color named Grant in Charleston in 1860, including Joseph Grant, a carpenter, Henry Grant, an umbrella manufacturer, and James Grant, a butcher. 1860 Population Schedule, Charleston, Ward 2, dwelling 133; Ward 2, dwelling 217; Ward 5, dwelling 329, SCDAH; *List of the Taxpayers of Charleston, 1860,* 324.

6. Fernando Wood, the mayor of New York City (not the governor of New York), was one of several candidates campaigning for a spot on the ticket of the national Democratic party. In an outdoor speech at the Mills House, Wood "referred to the intimate commercial and social relations existing between New York and Charleston, and said that in his person, the people of Charleston and of South Carolina, might receive assurances of continued amity. . . ." Charleston *Courier,* April 25, 1860; also, April 30, 1860.

7. Jim Lacoste was an old free man of color who worked as a wood factor. He did not pay any city property taxes or report any wealth to the federal census enumerator. 1860 Population Schedules, Charleston, Ward 6, dwelling 223, SCDAH.

8. The national convention of the Democratic party opened in Charleston on April 23, 1860. See letters of May 5, 1860, note 1 and May 14, 1860, note 2, below.

9. The Gilmore Brass Band of Boston accompanied the New England delegation to the Democratic Convention and gave numerous public concerts. Charleston *Mercury,* April 23, 1860.

10. On April 10, seventy-five additional policemen were added to the Charleston police force in anticipation of the convention crowds. The extra policemen were released on May 4. Charleston *Courier,* April 11, 1860; Charleston *Mercury,* May 5, 1860.

11. A local newspaper with a smaller circulation than either the *Courier* or the *Mercury,* according to the correspondent of the New York *Tribune,* November 10, 1860. Unfortunately, only a few scattered issues of the *Evening News* are extant.

Charleston, April 28th/60

Dear Henry,

We are glad to hear of your safe arrival. Your first letter did not reach when due. I am glad however that the Bundle was recovered. I was at the Depot Tuesday morn to send you Convention news. Failing to get the package off, I sent it Wednesday. Harriett Bonum[1] took it in charge. I have other papers but the Rain will prevent my getting them off. Beside there is no interesting news.

You will see by Friday's Mercury allusion made to words passed in the out door speeches made at Mills House.[2] It seems that Gen Schnierlie took exceptions to O Jennings Wise speech &, not satisfied with that, threatened to use his stick (so report says). A gent present tells of one speaker who got up & delivered himself thus, "What fools we are. Here we are in Convention & what is it all but Humbug, Humbug," & sat down. Allowance must be made for them that after imbibing hot punches, inhaling fresh air will confuse one's ideas.

W P. Dacoster[3] has disgraced his family by being so drunk on King St.[4] he had to be pulled thro the streets to the Guard House. This occured on Tuesday afternoon. The same night Mr Johnson,[5] Queen St, went to try & release him. After pleading some time with the officer, Lt Wilson,[6] he sent to have him brought out of the cell & he was then too drunk to appear. He got off with a Fine the next day & by 12 M was drunk again & has been so every day since. His Wife is to be pitied.

The Fireman's Parade was grand.[7] It was equal to the Torch light procession.[8] Their new engines made a gorgeous display. One was drawn by 4 horses richly caparisoned. A Fire broke out before they dismissed. A kitchen was burnt down.

The America raised [1100].[9] Neuffer & Saxon went on the cars & brought some down. The Mills had 1200, Charleston 600, Pavilion 3 or 400.[10] It is a perfect jam from the Institute Hall to Hibernian Hall[11] all day & night too I am told. The Boston Band,[12] it is said, refused $300 to play for the Fire Company. Their concert made them a fine yield.

Father, Mother, and the Family joins me in Love. As ever yrs truly

[Jas]

Mr. Henry Ellison
State Burg
Sumter District
So Ca

1. Harriet Bonum cannot be identified with certainty. She was probably a free woman of color who was related to the free man of color John Bonum, a huckster or street vendor in Charleston who paid no city property taxes although he reported owning real property worth $4,000 to the federal census marshal. 1860 Population Schedules, Charleston, Ward 4, dwelling 9, SCDAH.

2. Friday, April 27 the *Mercury* noted, "Public Meetings— Evening gatherings in front of hotels continue as largely attended as on previous nights. Last night a very large crowd gathered in front of the Mills House, and were addressed by Messrs. Gaulden of Georgia, O. J. Wise of Virginia, Gen. Schnierle of this city, and Judge Meek of Alabama. Some excitement, and a sharp passage of words, occurred at one period, but we trust that nothing serious will come of it."

3. William P. Dacoster (or Dacosta) was a free colored machinist who lived on Queen Street. In the 1850 federal census Dacoster's occupation was listed as "Cotton Gin Maker." In 1860 Dacoster paid city taxes on three slaves and real estate valued at $1,700. His immediate family included his wife Louise and at least six children. 1850 Population Schedules, Charleston, Ward 4, dwelling

51, and 1860 Population Schedules, Charleston, Ward 4, dwelling 15, SCDAH; *List of the Taxpayers of Charleston, 1860,* 318; Ford, *Census of Charleston, 1861,* 173.

4. King Street was the main retail thoroughfare in Charleston.

5. James Johnston, not Johnson, was a free man of color, a tailor, who lived on Queen Street near Dacoster. In 1860 Johnston paid city taxes on ten slaves and real estate worth $7,300. Johnston was married to a daughter of Thomas S. Bonneau, Eliza. Fitchett was incorrectly informed that Eliza Bonneau married James D. Johnson. Conclusive proof of this error is in the Free Negro Tax Books. The listings in the tax books were typically by family and each year between 1833 and 1841 James D. Johnson was listed with Delia Johnson. In 1836, 1837, 1839, and 1840 Eliza J. Bonneau was listed in the Bonneau family, although in 1840 "(now Johnson)" was listed after her name. In 1841 Eliza J. (Bonneau) Johnston was listed on Queen Street. *List of the Taxpayers of Charleston, 1860,* 325; Charleston Free Negro Tax Books, 1816–1846, SCDAH; Fitchett, "Free Negro in Charleston," 48; Ford, *Census of Charleston, 1861,* 171.

6. B. J. Wilson, a white man, was first lieutenant of the city

police. He boarded at the Planters Hotel at the corner of Church and Queen streets, very near the homes of Dacoster and Johnston. He paid no city property taxes in 1860. Ferslew, *Directory of Charleston, 1860*, 113, 148.

7. The annual parade of the ten fire companies was held on April 27, 1860. The parade was to be the first public trial of five new engines, but a fire alarm and the beginning of rain interrupted the parade and prevented the demonstration. Charleston *Mercury*, April 18 and 28, 1860.

8. The torch light parade of the city fire companies, complete with music, fireworks, and illuminated displays, had taken place on November 18, 1859, when Johnson was in Charleston. See letter of November 22, 1859, above. Charleston *Mer-*

cury, November 11 and 19, 1859.

9. The American Hotel, owned by the white persons G. A. and Mrs. M. L. Neuffer, was at the corner of King and George, directly across the street from James D. Johnson's tailor shop at 360 King. The letter apparently refers to the number of guests at the hotel. Ferslew, *Directory of Charleston, 1860*, 35.

10. The Mills, Charleston, and Pavilion were hotels, all of them located on Meeting Street. Again, the numbers apparently refer to the guests in each hotel. Ibid., 51, 108, 112.

11. Institute Hall, on the east side of Meeting Street, is about a block north of Hibernian Hall, on the west side of Meeting. Mills House is in between.

12. See letter of April 24, 1860, note 9, above.

Panama, New Granada,
South America
April 30/4/60

To My Esteemed Friends,[1]

It is now 17 years since I have left your little Borough.[2] *Would to God* I were there now. Had I of known as much as I know now I never should of left my *comfortable home*.

You are all aware of my Family's departing from our homes for the Island of Jamaica in May 1851, and perhaps this will be the [*first*] tidings that have ever reached you from us, although I wrote you all once from Jamaica and once from Aspinwall Navy Base N.G., of which I have never received any reply. But perhaps they never reached you. But as I have now a Favourable Opportunity, through the Politeness of Lieutenant Roberts of the U.S. Navy, I embrace the opportunity of writing once more. And should this reach you, Please give me all the news you can about the Family, [concerning] the prosperity of [*illegible word*] also how many Marriages & Deaths, of which I hope there is none of the latter. Also, how is Mr Natty[3] and Family and how many Children he has.

Now, as I have said, I wish I was back home. I have reason so to do, for you are aware that we were very comfortable there, and it seems as there has been a curse upon us every since we left home. I remained 2 years in Jamaica and then completely Failed. From thence my Father, Brother James, & myself came over here, leaving what little money we had with our Families. We were then employed by the Panama Rail Road Company as Overseers at $2.50 per day. My Poor Brother Died in 3 months after [he] was here and one month [*two illegible words*] I lost my then only Son, for you are aware that I lost one before I left home. I have now only one Daughter, near 10 years of age. My Poor unfortunate Father recieved an Injury whilst in the employ of the Said Company which has completely Disabled him for life. You you see the whole Burthen is thrown upon my Shoulders, and being in a country like this where every man is for himself, I find it *awfully hard* to get along. I see several ways that I could make money here, but not having anything like a capital, I can do nothing but Barbering and I can hardly pay my Rent and live out of it, having so many to feed and every thing is so very Dear here. As I have said, if I had a small Capital of $[200] make it [*illegible word*] in [*two illegible words*]. But I know of not a *Single Soul* in this world who would lend me the amount if I were to ask for it; so therefore I must be contented with my lot. Were it not for the misfortune of my Father Being Crippled, I could live very comfortably.

Now I suppose you all would like to know what sort of a place Jamaica is. Well in the first place, if you like Negro Company, you may go [*page or pages missing*]

[*Jack Thomas*]⁴

1. This letter was probably addressed to the Ellison family generally, but it was almost certainly designed to communicate with the elder William Ellison in particular.

2. A general reference to the Stateburg area.

3. While the census lists no one in Sumter District with the name Natty, it is possible that the writer was referring to Joseph M. Nettles or William Nettles, both older white planters with children. However, he may instead have been referring to a Sumter free man of color named Ignatius Miller. When Miller obtained a white guardian in December 1835, he noted his name thus: "Ignatius Miller (Natty Miller)." 1850 Population Schedules, Sumter, dwellings 641, 863, SCDAH; Sumter County Guardians of Free Blacks, 1823–1842, Sumter County Historical Society, Sumter, South Carolina. We are indebted to Mr. Esmond Howell for access to this unique document.

4. That Jack Thomas is the author is known because of the reference in James M. Johnson's letter of May 30, 1860, below. Thomas was almost certainly a free man of color who, as Johnson indicates, was forced to leave Stateburg because of some sort of serious incident.

Charleston, May 5th/60

Dear Henry,

Yours of 29th alt is duly Recd. I am happy to hear that All are well & that you Recd the package safe. I will send you a few more.

Your will learn ere this is recd of the adjournment of the Convention[1] & c. We are still busy. We have finished Dr Caldwell's[2] 2 suits to his satisfaction & have a lot on hand for his Brother Jas. Miss E Hampton[3] died on 3d inst. Her suitor Mr E White[4] is much affected.

I called on Mrs B[5] & to my surprise found that she had gone to Mrs Weston's.[6] I went up there and found her in good spirits. Faman[7] is in the Country. They were glad to hear that the Bundle were Recd, & was some relieved of their suspense as the Letter did not reach when due.

We are all tolerable. I will not elaborate as time is short. The Family joins me in Love.

W. P. D.[8] appears to be doing better. He enquired after you last Monday. He thought you were still down & hoped to see you again.

I have not seen many of the Ladies. The folks all think you are on the lookout, but you know best.[9] I have seen Miss Mary M[10] with her Beaux again. Whether it is a legal one or not, I do not know.

I must conclude with my best wishes for your health & happiness. Do before the Season passes get Old Moody[11] or Bynum Moore[12] to alter the colt So as he may Run at large. No more at present from yrs truly

J M Johnson

Mr H. Ellison
Attention
of J. T. Corbett, Esqr
Sumter

1. The Democratic Convention recessed on May 2, after the southern wing of the party had bolted and the remaining delegates were unable to agree on a nominee. They were to reconvene in Baltimore on June 18. Potter, *The Impending Crisis*, 407–12.

2. It has not been possible to identify Dr. Caldwell, but his brother James M. Caldwell, a white man, was a factor on North Atlantic Wharf and a large landholder in the Stateburg area. He paid municipal taxes on 12 slaves and real estate worth $4,000 and commissions of $23,000. Ferslew, *Directory of Charleston, 1860*, 48; *List of Taxpayers of Charleston, 1860*, 43; Miss Sadie M.

Caldwell to Anne King Gregorie, June 15, 1948, Anne King Gregorie Papers, SCHS.

3. Ellen Hampton was a free mulatto woman who was about 32 years old. 1850 Population Schedules, Charleston Neck, dwelling 570, SCDAH.

4. Edward White was a free mulatto carpenter who lived at 9 Kirkland Lane in 1859, almost next door to Ellen Hampton's residence at 13 Kirkland Lane. Means and Turnbull, *Charleston Directory, 1859*, 86, 221.

5. Jeanette Bonneau.

6. Louisa P. Weston, Mrs. Bonneau's daughter, lived on Henrietta Street, not far from The Citadel. Means and Turnbull, *Charleston Directory, 1859*, 220; Ford, *Census of Charleston, 1861*, 102.

7. Faman (or Furman) Weston was the husband of Louisa P. Weston. See letter of October 12, 1846, note 6, above.

8. William P. Dacoster. See letter of April 28, 1860, note 5, above.

9. Henry had not remarried since the death of his wife, Mary Elizabeth (Bonneau) Ellison, on September 15, 1852. Ellison family graveyard, Stateburg.

10. See letter of April 24, 1860, note 2, above.

11. Burrel Moody, a sixty-seven-year-old white planter, was a close neighbor of Johnson and the Ellisons in Stateburg. As early as 1833 and perhaps before, various members of the large Moody clan regularly employed William Ellison for blacksmithing and gin repairs. In the 1850s James M. Johnson made clothes for the Moody family. 1860 Population Schedules, Sumter, dwelling 691, SCDAH; Moody Family Papers, SCL.

12. See letter of January 20, 1860, note 12, above.

Grace Episcopal Church
From an original in the South Caroliniana Library.
Photograph by Charles Gay.

Charleston, May 14th/60

Dear Henry,

Your favor of 8th is recd & its varied contents noted. I am indebted to you for the full particulars in the melancholy occurrence at Swift Creek.[1] It was certainly an awful termination of a days hilarity.

I suppose ere this you are posted with regard to the action taken by the Convention to secure a nomination. The Seceders were awaiting the actions of the Nationals when they were Surprised by their adjournment without a nomination. They were cautious enough not to commit any overt act which would prevent their Return. Should the choice fall on a Candidate who embraces their views of [*or*] if the concessions they asked was granted, they would have gone back. As things were, they could only follow the Nationals & adjourn over to June.[2]

Messers Pollard, Kent,[3] & others from Georgia were here during the week. Mr W McK[4] gave a Supper.

You may have seen the Reception Hare[5] had at Kingsville in Wednesday's Mercury. He has been in so many Scrapes. It is no wonder he was identified.

The American[6] is about to go Smash. Neuffor is selling off his Liquors preparatory to an assignment. The larger Hotels may survive the Shock.

I am glad to hear from Mr Breck's[7] mission. I have the honor of perusing a letter of his to Mrs L P Weston[8] as Agt of Juvenile Society.[9]

I saw the Bishop[10] last week. He had the arm of a youth I presumed his Son, walking in King St. From his step and the motion of his eyes (he wore no glasses) I judge his vision was not altogether obscured.

I expect there will not be any call for an extra train to take candidates from Claremont up.

The present promises to be a week of great interest in the Church. Meetings are to be held every morning 6½ O'Clock at Grace Church.[11] I wish you would delegate yourself & come down & I will engage you will hear fine preaching, see fine Ladies, & if you will engage yourself away, to crown it their are 2 Maroons Monday & Music next by the Christian & Convivial Society. The annual address of the former is on Sunday next. I do further engage by way of inducement to Return Home with you in due time, provided the Ladies do not cause you to ground your arms & surrender for an indefinite period.

I was at Mrs Weston's[12] yesterday & such an array I have not seen in a private abode Recently. Mr R E D.[13] was there & so was Fred Sasportas.[14] Mr W[15] & Lady also Mr D[16] begs to be Remembered to you.

I did not see any of the Dacoster[17] Family at St Peters.[18]

I wished for you at the May Festival of the Germans at their Sporting ground.[19] Francis[20] & myself spent a very pleasant afternoon there. The crowd was immense & the Fun was of a novel & diverting kind. One chap[21] climbed the Greased Pole 50 ft high & got a watch. Several preceded him, but only to lose their labor & get where the prize looked more tempting as the view was nearer. The Turners in their Gymnastics could not be excelled by Equestrians in the same Feats. It was wound up by 2 locking & making their evolutions like a wheel Rocket. The Sharp Shooters were displaying their skill at the target & with the Tap of the Drum The Stout Lasses ran to the Dance.

It is a pity the May sport of the Sumterians came off with such Foul play.[22] It might have been a fruitful theme of public glorification for the Press, had it gone down with order & sobriety. It is to be feared, as Mr R[23] said, the Fire Water was there.

Mrs B[24] is at Mrs W[25] yet. She is well. Faman[26] is down.

We are busy at the Shop. Mr Jas Caldwell[27] has paid his Bill. He says he will Return to the Plantation soon. I joked him about gallanting the Ladies. He was quite pleased at it. Major Briggs was along & trying to persuade me to Return to Summerton;[28] regretted he did not know I was in Town so as he might have got his work done.

I cant come up to you. I must stop; if I have not repeated some thing old already, I will do so if I go on. The musquitoes are buzzing & I am oblivious to every thing else.

Father has been very unwell for a week. He is anxious to get off.[29] We are having letters weekly. Charley is going to Church, become a Teetotaller, & is happy in his new & enlarged House.[30] He only wants a heavier stock & that cannot be had without Money, which you know is scarce; cant you lend a helping hand. You will not lose it.

Mother is out at present. I have a cough. Father & the Family joins me in Love to your Honord Self, Father & Brothers. Yrs truly

J M Johnson

It is the Sister of Hampton[31] who married the [*illegible word*] who is dead. Gabriella visited her before she left & pronounced her case a hopeless one. She was engaged to E White who is much affected. (Hampton's wife[32] since her Death gave birth to a Stillborn Child.) The deceased was an amicable, intelligent Christian Woman, a Member of St Michaels.[33]

1. On May 5 a large group of young people went to Hamilton Boykin's Mill, on Swift Creek about 8 miles outside Camden, for a day-long picnic. About five o'clock in the afternoon, fifty or sixty persons—some with violins and guitars—got aboard a large flatboat and floated about fifty yards out into the mill pond, where the boat hit a snag. The boat sank in a few minutes. In the pandemonium, twenty-four persons drowned (later reports claimed twenty-seven), thirteen of them young white women, nine white men, and "two negroes." Charleston *Courier*, May 8 and 9, 1860; Charleston *Mercury*, May 9, 1860; *Sumter Watchman*, Extra, May 7, 1860; H. N. Roberts to Henry C. Burn, May 9, 1860, Burn Family Papers, SCL.

2. Johnson's description of the maneuvers and strategies of the southern Democrats is quite accurate. See Potter, *The Impending Crisis*, 407–412; Nichols, *The Disruption of American Democracy*, 288–308.

3. Pollard, Kent, and others were evidently free persons of color who lived in Georgia. William Pollard, a thirty-six-year-old free mulatto draymaster, was listed in the federal census in Savannah in 1860; he reported real estate worth $3,000 and personal property worth $600. No other free persons of color named Pollard or Kent appeared in the federal census

schedules for Savannah or Augusta in 1860. Although Savannah contained several free persons of color who were born in Charleston, William Pollard was born in Savannah. 1860 Population Schedules, Chatham County, Georgia, Savannah, Ward 1, dwelling 391, SCDAH. See also Sweat, "Free Negroes in Antebellum Georgia."

4. William McKinlay was a tailor, a member of the Brown Fellowship Society, and one of the wealthiest free men of color in Charleston. In 1860 he paid city taxes on real estate valued at $25,320. McKinlay lived on Coming Street, a few doors north of Mrs. Jeanette Bonneau. 1860 Population Schedules, Charleston, Ward 4, dwelling 477, SCDAH; Ford, *Census of Charleston, 1861*, 71; *List of the Taxpayers of Charleston, 1860*, 328.

5. According to an account from the Sumter *Watchman* for May 7, reprinted in the *Mercury* and the *Courier*, May 9:

A straggling fellow, (passing himself off as a white man, but believed to be a free negro) was soundly whipped at Kingsville yesterday, between two and three o'clock in the afternoon, by Mr. B. Franklin Cole, from the firm of Straus, Hartman, Hofflin & Co., of Baltimore.

Mr. Cole overheard Hare say that Maryland was an

Abolition State, in a boastful way. He immediately gave it the lie, and made towards him. Some words ensued, during which the true-hearted Baltimorean manfully stood his ground, and the straggler gave abundant evidence of his being an Abolitionist of the most low and dirty character. Soon it was suspicioned that he was but an impudent free negro from some Northern locality. This he acknowledged, upon being *pushed up* a little. Mr. Cole then took him aside, into an apartment of the Kingsville Hotel, made him *peel off*, and gave him the *limit* of the *law*, 'well filled, pressed down and shaken together,' upon his bare back.

Kingsville was a branch point on the railroad, about seventy miles northwest of Charleston.

6. The American Hotel, owned by Neuffer, was caught by surprise by the early adjournment of the Democratic Convention. See letter of April 28, 1860, notes 11 and 12, above.

7. J. Lloyd Breck was a white man, an Episcopal missionary to the Chippewa Indians in Minnesota. Each church took special collections for the support of his mission. In April 1860, the Juvenile Missionary Society of St. Paul's in Charleston gave $15.50 to his mission.

During the next month, a special collection was taken at Holy Cross in Stateburg and the children gave $11.45, the congregation, $90.00, and "negroes," $3.55, *Southern Episcopalian* 5 (April, 1858): 46–49; 7 (April, 1860): 55; 7 (May, 1860): 112.

8. Louisa Weston, Henry's sister-in-law.

9. Breck's letter probably thanked Mrs. Weston for the contributions of the Juvenile Society to his mission. See note 7, above.

10. Bishop Davis was afflicted with cataracts and was nearly blind. Late in May he went to Philadelphia for an operation to remove the cataracts and restore his vision. Charleston *Courier*, April 4, July 3, August 1, 1860. See letter of January 9, 1860, note 2, above.

11. During the convention of the Protestant Episcopal Church of South Carolina in Charleston, Grace Church held morning services. Charleston *Courier*, May 16, 1860.

12. It is impossible to be certain which Mrs. Weston Johnson was referring to. One possibility is Louisa P. Weston, the wife of Furman Weston. Another is Caroline Weston, the wife of Jacob Weston who lived next door to Mrs. Bonneau on Coming Street. He may have meant Harriet Weston, the wife of Samuel Weston, who lived

on Mazyck Street a few blocks south of Johnson's residence on Coming (Samuel and Jacob Weston ran a tailor shop on Queen Street), or he may have been referring to Maria Weston, the wife of Anthony Weston, a prominent free mulatto mill-wright who lived at the north-east corner of Calhoun and King near Johnson's tailor shop. Maria Weston was the wealthiest free person of color in Charleston, according to the city tax lists. In 1860 she paid city taxes on 14 slaves and real estate valued at $40,075. This information was public knowl-edge, since the city tax lists for 1859 and 1860 were published by the city council and dis-tributed free for the asking. 1860 Population Schedules, Charleston, Ward 4, dwellings 497, 161; Ward 5, dwelling 137, SCDAH; Ford, *Census of Charleston, 1861*, 51, 151; *List of the Taxpayers of Charleston, 1860*, 332.

13. Richard E. Dereef, a wood factor, was a member of the Brown Fellowship Society and one of the wealthiest free people of color in Charleston. Dereef, who was about sixty-two years old, paid municipal taxes on 14 slaves and real es-tate worth $23,000. 1860 Pop-ulation Schedules, Charleston, Ward 5, dwelling 592, SCDAH; *List of the Taxpayers of Charles-ton, 1860*, 319.

14. Frederick Sasportas was a well-known free mulatto mill-wright. In 1860 he paid city taxes on two slaves and real es-tate worth $2,000. 1860 Popu-lation Schedules, Charleston, Ward 8, dwelling 391, SCDAH; *List of the Taxpayers of Charleston, 1860*, 330.

15. Johnson was referring to one of the Westons, although it is impossible to be certain whether it was Furman, Jacob, Samuel, or Anthony. See note 12, above.

16. Richard E. Dereef. See note 13, above.

17. The family of William P. Dacoster, mentioned in previous letters. See letter of April 28, 1860, note 5; letter of May 5, 1860, note 8, above.

18. St. Peter's Protestant Episcopal Church was on Logan Street, between Broad and Tradd. Ferslew, *Directory of Charleston, 1860*, Appendix, 30.

19. The annual May Festival of the German Rifle Club and Turners' Association attracted hundreds of Charlestonians. The festival was held at the club's grounds on the outskirts of the city. On an eighteen-acre site, of which twelve acres were swamp, the club built a large two-story clubhouse, with a bar, billiard room, and bowling alley downstairs and a dance hall up-stairs. Ice cream and other re-freshments were available from tents pitched on the grounds. Sharpshooters took aim at an eagle target perched on a sixty-

foot pole one hundred yards away. Swings, a greased pole, gymnastic demonstrations, and other amusements were enjoyed by the crowds. The festival began May 2 and lasted for three days. The *Courier* praised the good order and decorum throughout the festival. Charleston *Mercury*, May 3, 5, 1860; Charleston *Courier*, May 3, 4, 5, 1860.

20. The identity of Francis cannot be positively established. It is most likely that Francis was a free man of color. He may well have been the free colored carpenter Francis M. Bonneau (whose relationship to the family of Thomas S. Bonneau has proved impossible to determine). Bonneau and James M. Johnson were about the same age and in 1850 Bonneau lived very near Johnson's father (James D. Johnson), perhaps next door. There are several other free men of color Johnson may have been referring to, including John L. Francis, who owned the property on King Street that housed James D. Johnson's tailor shop. However, it is also possible that Johnson was referring to Henry's sister-in-law, Frances Pinckney (Bonneau) Holloway. 1850 Population Schedules, Charleston, Ward 4, dwellings 413, 414, SCDAH; 1860 Population Schedules, Charleston, Ward 6, dwelling 332; Ward 4, dwelling 252,

SCDAH; Ford, *Census of Charleston, 1861*, 121; Means and Turnbull, *Charleston Directory, 1859*, 71, 107.

21. The *Courier* identified this "chap" as "a stalwart representative of young Africa." May 4, 1860.

22. Johnson was referring to the disaster at Swift Creek, which he mentioned at the beginning of this letter. See note 1, above.

23. The rumor that drinking had contributed to the panic that was responsible for the drownings was widespread. For example, H. N. Roberts wrote Henry C. Burn on May 9, 1860, "I am told that an abundance of Liquor was carried to the frolic, and that the Fiddle, Banjo, and Flute with skipping and dancing were going on at the moment [when the boat hit the snag]." It has proved impossible to identify "Mr R." Burn Family Papers, SCL.

24. Jeanette Bonneau.

25. Louisa P. Weston, Mrs. Bonneau's daughter.

26. Faman (or Furman) Weston, Louisa P. Weston's husband.

27. See letter of May 5, 1860, note 2, above.

28. Major Briggs cannot be positively identified, but Summerton was a small town in Clarendon District, about twenty miles south of Sumter.

29. James D. Johnson was

planning a trip to Canada to visit his son Charley. The trip figures in several subsequent letters.

30. Charley, his wife Gabriella, and his daughter Charlotte were the only residents in his two-story brick house at 36 Yonge Street West in Toronto. Canada West Census, 1861, Toronto, St. John's Ward, District 3, Reel 178, folio 598, PA.

31. Benjamin Hampton was the brother of Ellen Hampton, whose death Johnson had mentioned in the previous letter of May 5, 1860, note 3, above. Hampton was a free mulatto tailor about twenty-nine years old. He lived with his widowed mother Daphne, his sister Ellen, and his wife Sarah J., a milliner, at 13 Kirkland Lane,

just around the corner from Johnson's house on Coming. 1850 Population Schedules, Charleston, Ward 4, dwelling 379, and 1860 Population Schedules, Charleston, Ward 4, dwelling 666, SCDAH; Means and Turnbull, *Charleston Directory, 1859*, 86; Charleston Free Negro Tax Book, 1862, CLS; Ford, *Census of Charleston, 1861*, 107.

32. Sarah J. Hampton, the wife of Benjamin Hampton and the sister-in-law of the deceased Ellen Hampton.

33. St. Michael's Protestant Episcopal Church stood at the heart of the city at the corner of Broad and Meeting. It was a landmark of the Charleston skyline. Its spire housed bells that sounded curfew and alarms.

Charleston, May 21st/60

Dear Henry,

Your interesting epistle is at hand. I hasten to acknowledge the pleasure I found in its perusal. If not able to Reciprocate in the way of news, I shall be your confidant in the disclosures made, as I admire your frankness in unburdening yourself. And as Col Phillips[1] said to Col C G M,[2] it would perplex him[3] to answer his, Col P's, argument in the matter of Marriages among Slaves.[4] I confess it would me to controvert what you have adduced. I can only buoy you up by admonishing you as a Brother to be strong in the Spirit & you can obtain that Strength by Prayer alone. A widower[5] of 2 short yrs was, by trusting to his own strength, brought to feel his weakness. Having sworn to marry if first indulged, he then plead the terms he had allotted had not expired. His former Mother in Law gave him a release & told him to marry as his Honor was at Stake, if her daughter was not dead one year. The statue of limitation failing, she gave the Bride's friends & connections Mr Weston[6] as Leader & Brady & Oaks[7] as connections to take possession of her premises & use coercion. They did so & after confessing his intention to marry, asked to allow him to get through with the Maroon,[8] of which he was a Manager. Brady told him, Marry or Die, & sent for Dr Perrifoy[9] & to be doubly sure kept him, G,[10] under their eye, & posted off a Coach for the Bride who was nigh so that poor G had no chance to Fly. And as he could show no cause Why the Knot should not have an immediate tie, he was made to verify what he meant for a lie & [*that*] will learn him next time to Marry & then *Try*. Poor foolish Girl, all she did was to cry. But perhaps she will have a Baby Bye & Bye, & if he dont feed it, she may blame her Hurry. She is a Miss Leman,[11] & strange to say I saw her today. She was married yesterday afternoon & that must satisfy.

As Miss J. Lee[12] remarked at the shop door (while I was reading your letter) in reply to a female who told her she would be the next in the Family to go off, "Oh no," she said, "I am satisfied." "Yes," said the friend, "That's True." I heard every word. It was near 8 o'clock P.M. & Grant[13] was at the door. He thought she had a hard cheek to confess to that & look at him & laugh. I saw her go up in the afternoon & went out & saw from the Gas light it was her. She has stopped going to Church since her Suitor's Return & I have not seen her out since Febry.

Hare[14] is a Brother of the one you alluded to & was in that affair with the stolen corpse in Georgetown.

I saw Mr D[15] today & was invited to ride up with him, but I was too busy. I will go up when I get leisure. I heard a married man speaking highly of their Ladies & their agreeable beauty, in contrast with Washington St,[16] when he is on the most intimate terms with the males.

I heard McCready[17] silenced by Col Calhoun[18] in reply to his sarcasm about the convention being held in Abbeville. He is a portly man & reminds me of Gov P M Butler[19] in his [address].

It is 12 at night, my pen & eyes are failing, the musquitoes are on duty, & I must retire. We have 2 suits for Dr Thomson[20] of Sumter. I saw Mr H L P[21] at convention one day. I had no time to stay but when Col P[22] got the floor I could not get away. I am with the [love of] Father and the Family

As ever
J M Johnson

1. Col. John Phillips, a white man, was a delegate from Christ Church Parish to the recently concluded Diocesan Convention of the Protestant Episcopal Church of South Carolina that had been held in Charleston. Charleston *Courier*, May 18, 19, 1860.

2. Christopher G. Memminger was also a delegate to the diocesan convention. Memminger chaired a committee appointed by the 1858 convention "to consider and report under what circumstances a clergyman may unite slaves in marriage," in the words of the committee's report, which had been submitted to the 1859 session of the convention. The highly controversial report was carried over to the 1860 convention, where it was the subject of heated debate, with Col. Phillips leading the opposition. The committee report argued that as "the mar-

riage relation between slaves has the same divine obligation as between masters and mistresses," the "duty of every Christian master is thus ascertained with the certainty which attaches to divine precepts. He is bound to preserve inviolate the marriage tie between his slaves, and to prevent, as far as in him lies, the separation of husband and wife." On the whole, the report continued, Christian masters obeyed these dictates, but "among masters who do not recognize the force of Christian obligation, there will be abuses," in particular the forced, involuntary separation of slave husbands and wives. In such instances, the committee found upon surveying the clergy of the diocese, there was "a general concurrence in the practice of allowing marriages, in cases where the parties have been separated in such a way as to

render impossible the fulfill-
ment of the marriage obliga-
tions." The committee proposed
a series of resolutions on the
question which it did not intend
"to clothe with the sanction of
Law, but simply to announce as
the opinion of the convention."
Essentially, the resolutions proposed that current diocesan
practice be made policy, that
slaves who had been forcibly
and involuntarily separated from
their spouses should be allowed
by the church to remarry. By
itself, this proposition was probably unobjectionable to the convention. The intensity of the
opposition can be appreciated
by considering the language
of the first three resolutions
and then the critical seventh
resolution:

> 1. *Resolved*, That the rela-
> tion of husband and wife is of
> divine institution, and the du-
> ties which appertain to it are
> of universal obligation, and
> bind with the same force the
> master and the slave.
> 2. That the injunction of
> our Savior forbidding man to
> separate those whom God has
> joined together, is obligatory
> upon the conscience of every
> Christian master, and pro-
> hibits the separation of those
> who have been united in
> marriage.
> 3. That the power over
> the slave, which is conferred
> upon the master by the law of

the land, should be exercised
by every Christian in conformity with the law of God;
and therefore, every Christian
master should so regulate the
sale and disposal of a married
slave, as not to infringe the
Divine injunction forbidding
the separation of husband and
wife. . . .
> 7. That where an involun-
> tary and final separation of
> married slaves has occurred,
> the case of the sufferers [the
> slaves] is to be distinguished
> from any human agency
> which has separated them.
> The latter [the master] is re-
> sponsible to God for dis-
> regarding his commands; the
> former are entitled to sympa-
> thy and consideration.

As the opposition quickly
sensed, the committee's report
identified the root of the problem as masters who did not
"recognize the force of Christian
obligation." The text of the
report was published in the
Charleston *Courier*, May 13,
1859. The debate in the 1860
convention was reported in the
Courier, May 19, 1860.
3. Memminger.
4. Phillips argued that adop-
tion of the Memminger report
would produce "discord" in
the councils of the Episcopal
Church in the United States,
would invite interference by
northerners in the affairs of
South Carolina, and most im-

portant of all would have the force of a pronouncement of law by the convention. "What is that law?" he asked. "It recognizes upon the Christian master that the contract which his slave makes shall be valid and obligatory. Are we prepared for that? Are we prepared to say that a slave can make a contract? Your law does not. Your State law does not. He understood when the voice of God is heard, that it overrides all human law, but he was not to be persuaded into the idea that it was reasonable to force the Church into an antagonistic position to the State." The opponents of the committee report offered three substitute resolutions that cast the divine injunction somewhat differently:

> *Resolved*, That as the relation of master and servant, as well as that of husband and wife, is a Divine appointment, and is thus recognized throughout the Recorded Will of God, there can be no necessary conflict between the conduct of a Christian master, and the rights and obligations arising out of the relationship of married slaves.
>
> *Resolved*, That the evil of separating husband and wife, arises not necessarily from the institution of domestic slavery, but like all other evils incident to every form of human society, is the result of

the fallen condition of man; and that, in point of fact, this evil so far from being peculiar to the institution, has been mitigated and restrained by the authority of the Christian master, and, for its complete removal, required not any interposition of the Church, except in the reformation and Christianization of mankind.

> *Resolved*, That the Church in the Diocese of South Carolina now, as it always has, regards it as the imperative duty of the Christian master to observe the injunction of our Savior, forbidding man to separate those whom God has joined together, and in this, as in all other respects, to govern his slaves in strict conformity to the laws of God.

The convention ultimately tabled the substitute resolutions and the committee report. The controversy was not dead, however. A member of the committee attacked Phillips's arguments in a series of letters published in the *Courier*, each of which was answered by a supporter of Phillips. See A. W. to Editor, Charleston *Courier*, May 29, July 2, 14, 1860; S. to Editor, *Courier*, June 13, July 2, 26, 1860. Phillips's remarks were published in the *Courier*, May 19, 1860.

5. In his next letter (May 30, 1860) Johnson identified the widower as Rixy Gordon. Gor-

don, whose real name was James, was a free mulatto about twenty-one years old who worked as a butcher. In 1860 he paid city taxes on real estate worth $1,400. Charleston Free Negro Tax Book, 1860, Carter G. Woodson Papers, LC; Charleston Free Negro Tax Book, 1862, CLS; *List of the Taxpayers of Charleston, 1860*, 109.

6. The mother of Gordon's former wife (now dead) gave the friends and connections of the bride-to-be (Christiana Leman) the name of Mr. Weston as leader. Although it is not certain, Mr. Weston was probably one of the prominent free men of color—Anthony, Samuel, or Jacob Weston. Being "Leader" probably entailed serving as an intermediary for the young free woman of color in the negotiations and arrangements with Gordon's former mother-in-law (and her friends and connections) for the impending shotgun marriage.

7. Brady and Oaks were the enforcers for Gordon's former mother-in-law. Both were free men of color with little property. Francis Brady paid municipal taxes on a horse; Samuel B. Oakes, a thirty-year-old bootmaker, paid no city taxes because he lived just outside the city limits, but he reported to the federal census personal property worth $200. Charles-

ton Free Negro Tax Book, 1857, SCDAH; *List of the Taxpayers of Charleston, 1860*, 316; 1860 Population Schedules, Christ Church Parish, dwelling 124, SCDAH.

8. A maroon was a picnic in the country, usually accompanied by music, dancing, and general merriment. A good example is the German May Festival discussed in the letter of May 14, 1860, above. Fire companies, militia units, and other organizations held maroons throughout the month of May. It has proved impossible to identify the maroon Gordon was managing. For more on the maroon, see the next letter, below.

9. Archibald Pierifoy (or Peurifoy) was a white Methodist minister who was over sixty years old. He paid city taxes on six slaves held in trust for his children, according to a note in the federal census. 1860 Population Schedules, Charleston, Ward 6, dwelling 239, SCDAH; *List of the Taxpayers of Charleston, 1860*, 221.

10. Rixy Gordon.

11. Christiana Leman was listed in the federal census as an eighteen-year-old free mulatto mantua maker, who lived with Mary Gibbes, 37, another mantua maker. 1860 Population Schedules, Charleston, Ward 5, dwelling 183, SCDAH; Charleston Free Negro Tax Book,

1860, Carter G. Woodson Papers, LC.

12. Josephine Lee was the nineteen-year-old daughter of the prominent free colored steward, John Lee. For information about John Lee see the letter of August 20, 1860, note 17, below. 1860 Population Schedules, Charleston, Ward 4, dwelling 243, SCDAH.

13. Grant was probably a slave who belonged to James D. Johnson. See the letter of April 24, 1860, note 5, above.

14. Hare was the free man of color who was whipped in Kingsville, mentioned in the letter of May 14, 1860, note 5, above. His brother may have been Stephen H. Hare, a free mulatto tailor in his late twenties who lived on Magazine Street, just around the corner from the tailor shop of Samuel and Jacob Weston on Queen Street. Ford, *Census of Charleston, 1861*, 135; Charleston Free Negro Tax Book, 1862, CLS.

15. Joseph Dereef was a prominent member of the free colored community in Charleston. He belonged to the Brown Fellowship Society and was among the wealthiest free people of color in the city. In 1860 he paid city taxes on six slaves and real estate valued at $16,000. He lived on Amherst Street in the northeast part of the city, a fair distance from Johnson's shop on King Street.

Like his brother Richard, he was a wood factor. 1860 Population Schedules, Charleston, Ward 7, dwelling 219, SCDAH; *List of the Taxpayers of Charleston, 1860*, 319; Ford, *Census of Charleston, 1861*, 32.

16. The contrast was between the ladies in Joseph Dereef's household—among them two eligible young women —and those in the household of Richard E. Dereef, who lived on Washington Street. Same sources as note 15, above, except Ford, *Census of Charleston, 1861*, 215.

17. Edward McCrady was one of several delegates to the Diocesan Convention who opposed holding the next convention in the remote upcountry village of Abbeville. Charleston *Courier*, May 18 and 19, 1860.

18. According to a report in the *Courier* (May 19, 1860), J. A. Calhoun said "that as a representative of Abbeville, he could say that they had a great desire to see the Convention at that place. He thought it would be for the interest of the Church that there should be, once in a while at least, a Convention of the Episcopal Church held in the upper part of the State."

19. Pierce Mason Butler was born in upcountry Edgefield District in 1798, settled in Columbia where he became president of the state bank of South Carolina, and was elected gover-

nor of the state in 1836. Colonel of the Palmetto Regiment in the Mexican War, he was killed in 1847 at the battle of Churubusco. *Dictionary of American Biography*, s.v. "Butler, Pierce."

20. Dr. Thomson cannot be identified with certainty; most likely he was a white resident of the town of Sumter.

21. H. L. Pinckney, Jr., was a white man who was a delegate to the Diocesan Convention from Claremont Parish, representing the Church of the Holy Cross, Stateburg, where the Ellisons and Johnson were members. William Ellison's white guardian, Dr. W. W. Anderson, was also a delegate to the convention. Charleston *Courier*, May 18, 1860.

22. Col. Phillips, mentioned at the beginning of this letter. See notes 1 and 4, above.

Charleston, May 30th/60

Dear Henry,

Yours is recd. I must disabuse you as to the supposed error in your allusions. I have too much faith in your consistency to suspect you would allow your passions to betray you into any act implicating [*illegible name*].[1] And I did not intend the notice to the Leman & Gordon case to have the least connection either by way of comparison or analogy. I certainly intended however to give you the names of the party as I had it, Christina Leman vs Rixy Gordon. The circumstances under which I wrote must plead my excuse for errors & confusion of ideas & I am sorry to add, I find myself under the same now. But I must attempt to Reciprocate your attention full as I may. I must digress from the case above cited as there are so many contradictory tales of the issues that it would be Requisite to give them all & have you form an opinion & to do that would require a manuscript of a few sheets of Foolscap (apropos by the way) & I must await further developments with the hope to be enabled to give you still greater detail verbatim.

And now is the Time to answer your question when do I expect to come up. I am forced to say I cannot be definite. It may be in a week or not for a fortnight. I did expect to get off the last of the month, but if I did so, it would be to the neglect of business & my stay could only be for a few days & I think it best to tarry until I can be spared longer. Should you have any commands, forward them forthwith in case I conclude to break though all obstacles & come off before I have time to notify you.

The Maroon[2] came off extra fine Thursday. I was up Town soon after 5 A.M. & saw some of the Ladies on their way to the starting point of the stages, omnibuses, &c. & soon after met *Rixy* shopping. He was minus a cravat & perhaps was getting a fancy one. He was the gayest of the gay at the Maroon. Christina I saw last of all wending her way to work. She is said to be all attention & excuses herself in visiting with, "I must go, I have my Husband's Dinner to get." And, ungrateful wretch, he says she isn't Mrs G & wont feed the Baby. Kalb[3] will have to be called. This hard case is like McBeth's Ghost, wont be dismissed. But as a finale I will lay it with the Parson. I saw Peirrifoy[4] twice today & he is used up—pale & emaciated. Those Bull Dogs have scared him badly (Brady & Oakes).[5]

Their crew had a Maroon[6] today and you may expect in the next quotations to find the Liquor Market at high figures & none on hand. Garrett[7] had a Coach with some Children inside on their Return & himself full & a champagne basket outside. He looked like a cask & methinks a tapping would have caused a rise to set the coach afloat. Ben Kinloch[8] & Bill Marsh[9] all was there & you may know the Corn Juice was at a Premium. The spring carts went up loaded with the Luxuries & was seen coming down early with the Tables &c. Alas, it was too soon transferred to copper fastened vessels made of Flesh although they be.

And now I must say a word for the Ladies in Amherst St.[10] I would be happy to have it in my power to Recommend them by experience, but my present circumstances debar me from even indulging the hope that I could do so. By desultory visits, from observations, & the confirmation of interested parties I pronounce them as models. I visit so little that it would be unfair for me to do so to the disparagement of others not less worthy. And as you look forward to another Term of Matrimonial Life, I bid you God speed & would have you untrammelled in your choice when the Time comes. I hold it to be a personal affair, not subject to dictations & with proper precautions on your part, viz to seek to find out whether the disposition & character of the object is adapted to your own before concentrating your affections. And whatever regard a man's taste may prompt him to entertain for beauty, form, &c. in seeking a bosom companion for Life, let him see to it that his predilections does not bias him to sacrifice the substance to the shadow. For what else is beauty & form & where is the substance if not assimilated to a kind & gentle disposition & a loving Heart. And where is this to be found but in the Christian Ladies.

I am agreeably surprised to hear of Jack Thomas' Epistle.[11] He has to keep his eyes open now when asleep. I presume the Time was when he closed them, when awakened with the prospect of an abundant final siesta. I wish he was at the Borough[12] once more. It was his adventures with poor Natty[13] in that way recalls him most. I would not like to risk a Wagon on a Gross, I think he was gorged then with a half. But I will not trifle thus with a serious matter. I just heard tonight after receiving your letter his sister is married to Mr Wm Tardiff[14] of Chstn & gone to California. His mother is living with Mrs Tardiff.

I cannot speak with any certainty as to Father's leaving. He is much better and willing to come up. He is very anxious to leave & says the needful is all that will keep him. He cant get rid of his pest[15] or he would go very soon. She is in the Broker's hands.

We have not heard or written to Canada since you wrote me. I should have in my last adverted to your remarks in the matter of Charley. I feel assured so far as friendly relations go, if you can overlook his delinquency, he would readily confess & it may be, forsake his neglect. But in epistolary correspondence when a man feels that he has done violence to a friend by too long neglect he feels also that it is irretrievable until allowed otherwise. Father, Mother, and the family joins me in love.

J M Johnson

1. All that can be said with certainty is that the name begins with the letter H.

2. Neither the *Mercury* nor the *Courier* mentioned a maroon that was held on Thursday, May 24. The Charleston Fire Company celebrated a maroon on the twenty-second and the German Fire Company's maroon was on the twenty-third. Perhaps Johnson was referring to one of these and was incorrect about the date. Or just as likely the maroon he was referring to, which evidently involved many (and perhaps only) free persons of color, was not reported in the local newspapers. Charleston *Courier*, May 24, 1860; Charleston *Mercury*, May 23, 24, 1860.

3. Probably Jacob H. Kalb, a wealthy white man who lived at 30 Rutledge Street, not far from Johnson's residence on Coming. Kalb paid city taxes on seven slaves, a horse and carriage, and real estate valued at $37,000. Kalb's relationship to the principals in the Leman–Gordon affair is not clear. In any case, Rixy and Christiana worked out their differences since, according to Fitchett, they eventually had three daughters and a son. Ford, *Census of Charleston,*

1861, 181; *List of the Taxpayers of Charleston, 1860*, 147; 1860 Population Schedules, Charleston, Ward 6, dwelling 607, SCDAH; Fitchett, "The Free Negro in Charleston," diagram following 183.

4. The Methodist minister; see the letter of May 21, 1860, note 9, above.

5. The men who forced Gordon to marry Leman; see the previous letter, note 7, above.

6. The maroon was evidently held by a group of free men of color.

7. Probably Samuel Garrett, a free man listed in the 1860 federal census as black rather than mulatto. Garrett was a tailor and owned no property, according to the census listing. 1860 Population Schedules, Charleston, Ward 5, dwelling 156, SCDAH.

8. Benjamin K. Kinloch was a forty-one-year-old free mulatto millwright of modest means. He paid municipal taxes on one horse and reported to the federal census personal property worth $500. 1860 Population Schedules, Charleston, Ward 4, dwelling 476, SCDAH.

9. Johnson was probably referring to William Marshall, a thirty-two-year-old free mulatto

barber who lived at 50 Coming Street, as did Kinloch. 1860 Population Schedules, Charleston, Ward 4, dwelling 476, SCDAH; Charleston Free Negro Tax Book, 1860, Carter G. Woodson Papers, LC.

10. Elizabeth and Abbey Dereef, daughters of Joseph Dereef, were, respectively, twenty-four and eighteen years old in 1860, according to the federal census. As noted in the letter of May 21, 1860, note 15 above, Joseph Dereef and his family lived on Amherst Street. 1850 Population Schedules, Charleston Neck, dwelling 673, and 1860 Population Schedules, Charleston, Ward 7, dwelling 219, SCDAH.

11. Johnson was referring to the letter of April 30, 1860, above.

12. Stateburg.

13. Thomas had inquired about Natty in his letter to the Ellisons of April 30, 1860.

14. William Tardiff was probably the son of the free man of color by the same name who joined the Brown Fellowship Society in 1830. After the elder Tardiff's death sometime before 1844, his wife Elizabeth continued to live in Charleston with her children. "Members of the Brown Fellowship Society," RSSL; 1850 Population Schedules, Charleston Neck, dwelling 49, SCDAH; Charleston Free Negro Tax Book, 1857, SCDAH; Charleston Free Negro Tax Book, 1860, Carter G. Woodson Papers, LC.

15. James D. Johnson was trying to sell an expensive gun. See letter of August 4, 1860, note 3, below.

Charleston, Aug 4th [*1860*]

Dear Henry,

I am grateful for your promptness & regret that I cannot carry out your requests by default of express. Their delay has fermented the preserves & rashness has spilt the Honey & with the spoiling of the grapes it was a pickle pie. I know your kind intentions will be appreciated & will carry with me your kind wishes. Please say to my Friend Wm[1] I am also obliged to him.

I cannot answer either of your fine letters. Suffice it to say I thank you both for your good wishes & hope we may be spared to see each other again & renew past pleasures.[2]

By the way, My Worthy Friend, before I got yours I had sold my gun[3] for $1000 less some $100 for expenses. It is said to be the best sale had in that Market & the Broker Wagers a Fine Over Coat if it is demurred to. Say no more about bad speculating until you hear she is on hand again. I am your obt [servt]

J. D. Johnson

P S. Paper spoilt. I will get the leather up on Tuesday. If I do not get off myself, do as you may no [*illegible word*] for nothing. Will you please send to the Depot [*four or five illegible words*] Yours truly

J M Johnson

1. William Ellison, Jr.

2. James D. Johnson was about to leave on a trip to visit Charley in Canada. State laws passed in 1822 and 1835 prohibited any free person of color who left the state from ever returning. Those who did return were subject to seizure and trial before a magistrate's court. If convicted, an offender had fifteen days to leave the state. If the person did not comply, he or she was subject to such corporal punishment as the magistrate's court directed. If the person did not leave the state within fifteen days after being punished and was so convicted by a magistrate's court, he or she could then be sold as a slave, with half the proceeds going to the state, the other half to the informer. The laws were not strictly enforced in the late 1850s, as the letters in this collection make clear. Free people of color traveled at will from South Carolina to New York and to Canada. But when the secession crisis intensified in August 1860, the law began to be enforced, as subsequent letters disclose. O'Neall, *The Negro Law of South Carolina*, 15–16.

3. Delay in the sale of this gun had caused Johnson to postpone his trip. See letter of May 30, note 15, above.

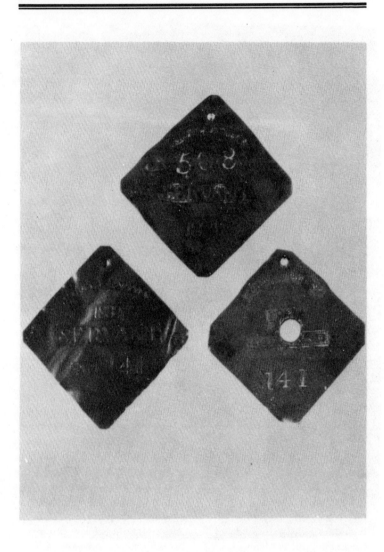

Slave Badges
These badges are in the collections of the McKissick Museum of the
University of South Carolina and the State Museum of South Carolina.
Photograph by Charles Gay.

                                   Charleston Aug 20th 1860
Dear Henry,

   Since my absence the agitation has been so great to cause many to
leave who were liable to the law of 1822 & the panic has reached
those whom that law cannot affect.[1] I was at Mr Jos Dereef[2] last
night & he seems to be more oppressed than any one I have spoken
with. He cites the case of a Female whose Grandmother he knew to
be Bona fide[3] & knew her Mother also, when she had this child. She
came to him to identify her, he being the only person that knew her
origin that she could refer to & he could not relieve her[4] & there are
numbers in the same dilemma. It is such cases that awaken sympathy. There are cases of persons who for 30 yrs have been paying capitation Tax[5] & one of 35 yrs that have to go back to bondage & take
out their Badges,[6] & for the consolation of those who are exempt[7] we
are told this is the beginning. The next session[8] will wind up the
affairs of every free cold. man & they will be made to leave. Those
who are now hunted down have divined what is to be done with
them & before their destiny is sealed by an amendment[9] are wisely
leaving by every Steamer & Railroad too. The Keystone State[10]
takes out several to day. Their friends & counsellors[11] tell them to
leave. The time is at hand when none may remain but them[12] & their
slaves. They[13] have taken the advice as they are to be embraced in
the latter.

   A Cold. Lady now North left a servt at Home[14] to take care of her
place. Her friend a lawyer is applied to. He says the Servt must have
a Badge & the Lady who he will do any thing for, must make up her
mind to stay, as no mortal man will be allowed to return.[15] The Dereefs have had to pay some $80 fines, for Servts without Badges.[16] I
saw Mr Jon Lee[17] going down to Stmr to get off Demar's[18] wife &
Matthews[19] *children*. He says it is plain now all must go & his
Brother[20] is of the same opinion. *Great change.*

   The higher class[21] is quite incensed but it is too late. The power is
into other hands[22] & when they have got rid of the cold. population
they will try to make them[23] subordinate. Of the many hundred perhaps thousand cases before the court represented by Lawyers &
Gentlemen of standing, but one or two have stood suit & they are for
persons lately freed.[24]

   They have not visited Coming St.[25] as yet, but have declared their
intention not to leave one family uncalled upon. I am glad I am here
for the many reports with the startling facts require some one in
every house to allay the excitement. Aspinall's partner is not clear[26]
& he is next to Mr Dereef,[27] but he will go in Queen St.[28] seeking

comfort. It is beyond doubt that it will kill many. It is like the heat of this summer conceded to be the hottest & most deadly assault ever made upon this class, & animal, like vegetable life, must wither & die from the shock. God grant them a joyful resurrection.

I heard in the cars[29] that Petitions are drawn & handed around for signatures by Country Members[30] to sell those[31] there who are considered worthless, prior to passing a Law for the removal of the Body. They[32] of the country are [seen] to be equal to Bears at stealing corn & the present [short] supply will be a motive to appropriate them[33] as How to make a larger crop next year.

Mr Verree[34] has made up his mind to leave. Do acquaint your Father of the state of feeling. It is a State law,[35] & to use the expression of those who have the matter in hands "What is to come will be worse." When that comes every property holder will be glad to take what he can get (irrespective of value) for his property.

Among those leaving by N Y strm was a white cold. woman who with her children was put ashore.[36] Her Baggage could not be got at. The Capt. is to take care of it at N Y. She was not arrested at all.

Poor Browne that Andrews[37] shot died in N Y. It is hinted to be suicide. He was awfully mortified.

Isham Moore[38] came down from Summerville[39] Friday. He says they have parties every night, & live as well as in the City. He left a Brag Cotton Crop at Home. Mr. Griffin of Texas hired 300 acres & did not make a single ear of corn. The entire crop failed. He says corn can be made in a drought by frequent working. He was to go up Home to day.

Miss Mary Dereef[40] is gone to Anderson Court House.[41] It is Miss Abby Dereef[42] that Mr Anderson[43] goes Courting, so I was right & hence the mistake as you may see above. Miss Jessie[44] is as blooming as ever. They are eager to leave & if you know of a worthy fellow who feels like emigrating you can recommend him. So as they are in good company it dont matter if they are bound to the State of Matrimony & by the [*two illegible words*] if it is preferable.

Father[45] was fortunate in meeting H B Lee[46] as soon as he left the ship in search of a Barber. He had just got the notice & was going to the Ship. He left the same evening by Portland & Montreal route[47] & arrived on Friday at Canada. He is delighted with the Sights. Miss Merrill[48] goes soon.

Leslie is quite happy again. Mrs Bonneau is well as usual. She sends her Love & thanks for the Grapes & wishes to know if you speak of coming down. If you dont come soon you wont find that number of Ladies to select from you enumerated not long since.

They are juicing down (reducing) very fast. Give my Love to All at Wisdom Hall & accept for yourself the same. Yrs truly

J M Johnson

1. In December 1822, the state legislature passed "An Act for the Better Regulation and Government of Free Negroes and persons of Color." The law was a direct response to the most elaborate slave insurrection conspiracy in American history. The leader of the conspiracy was Denmark Vesey, a free black carpenter in Charleston. With the help of a few influential slaves who worked as skilled tradesmen in the city, Vesey tried to organize a general slave uprising to seize Charleston and murder whites. Set for mid-July, the plan was foiled when a slave—on the advice of a free man of color—informed his master what was afoot. Authorities acted quickly to root out the conspiracy, and by mid-August thirty-five blacks had been executed and more than thirty others deported. The legislature designed the 1822 law to prevent such a conspiracy in the future.

The provision of the 1822 law that caused the panic Johnson referred to required every free man of color to have a white guardian who was a "respectable freeholder" in the district where he resided. The guardian was to appear before the clerk of court in his district

and testify to the "good character and correct habits" of the free man of color and record his acceptance of the guardianship. According to the law, any free man of color who failed to obtain a white guardian was to be sold as a slave, one-half of the proceeds to go to the informer, the other half to the state. Obviously, every well-advised free man of color complied with the law. But within a few years white vigilance abated and the law was indifferently enforced. In the decades after 1822 many free persons of color failed to obtain a white guardian or, if they did make a guardianship agreement with a white man, they failed to register it with the clerk of court. In August 1860, as Johnson put it, those persons were "liable to the law of 1822." That is, if they could not prove they had a white guardian who was registered with the clerk of court, they were subject to be sold as slaves.

Complicating this relatively simple question was another form of guardianship or trusteeship that had evolved as a legal dodge of an 1820 state law prohibiting masters from emancipating their slaves. Although the law stated that "no slave shall hereafter be emancipated but by an act of the Legislature," hundreds of South Carolina slaveholders continued to want to manumit one or more favored slaves and sought a way around the law. The result, as Judge John Belton O'Neall wrote in 1848, was "evasions without number." In the debate on slave marriages in the Episcopal convention in May 1860, Colonel John Phillips noted that experienced lawyers were often asked "how the law may be defeated by leaving slaves free." The legal device used was a deed of trust. A slaveowner could vest the ownership of a favored slave in a trustee, who was required by the terms of the trust to allow the slave to live as a free person.

William Ellison himself had used this legal device to effect the freedom of his daughter Maria. On November 17, 1830, Ellison purchased Maria from her owner, Dr. David J. Means of Winnsboro, "with a view to procur & affect her emancipation." The next day Ellison recorded a deed of trust, documenting his sale of Maria for one cent to Colonel William McCreight, the white man he had served as an apprentice gin-maker when he was a slave twenty years earlier. According to the deed, Ellison acted "in consideration of the love and affection which I have for my natural daughter Maria, a woman of colour." The terms and conditions of the trust established Maria's de facto freedom: Maria could live with Ellison or "whomever he directs"; Ellison reserved the right to emancipate her at any future time in South Carolina, if that were to become possible, or in another state; upon Ellison's death, McCreight was to "secure her emancipation as soon as possible" in South Carolina or elsewhere, the expenses to be borne by Ellison's estate without contest by his executors; neither McCreight nor his heirs were to have any right to the services of Maria; and all of these conditions were to extend to any children born to her. In effect, Maria was as free as a slave could become in South Carolina after 1820. And indeed she lived as a free woman of color in Fairfield District, the wife of Henry Jacobs, a free mulatto carriage maker. Nonetheless, Maria remained a slave in the eyes of the law.

Hundreds of other "free" persons of color were in Maria's situation. They had a white guardian in the form of the person who owned them in trust. They lived as free persons and complied with the laws governing free persons of color. But technically they were still slaves. These individuals were, in Johnson's words, "liable to the law of 1822" with a special twist. They stood to lose all rights guaranteed to them by the trusts under which they were held and the children of all the women in this status became slaves. The decision of Charleston authorities to insist on rigid enforcement of the 1820 and 1822 laws left the free colored community panic-stricken, for good reason. McCord, *Statutes at Large*, vol. 7, 459–62; Kennedy and Parker, *An Official Report*; O'Neall, *Negro Law of South Carolina*, 11; Charleston *Courier*, May 19, 1860; South Carolina Miscellaneous Records, Book G, 231–33, SCDAH; 1850 Population Schedules, Fairfield District, dwelling 234, SCDAH.

2. Although Joseph Dereef, like his brother Richard, was an "Indian" rather than a "mulatto," he was nonetheless a "free man of color." Neither "Indian" nor "mulatto" was precisely defined or used, but "mulatto" indicated a mixture of white and black ancestors, "Indian" a mixture of white and Indian. Skin color, of course, was not a reliable guide to ancestry. Dereef's free status was beyond doubt, but he was "oppressed" because of what was happening to other free persons of color.

3. That is, the grandmother was free before 1820, when manumission was prohibited by a state law. (See note 1, above.) Since the status of a child was determined by the status of its mother, the grandmother's "bona fide" free status legally conferred free status on the mother, who in turn passed it on to *her* daughter, the woman who came to see Dereef. The woman's problem was that she could not prove she was free. As a woman of color she was presumed to be a slave unless she could prove otherwise. Since the woman was probably born after 1820, the presumption that she was a slave was especially strong, unless the free status of her mother could be established. That required documentary evidence that her mother was either manumitted before 1820 or freeborn, in which case the free status of *her* mother (the grandmother of the woman who came to Dereef) was at issue. The woman apparently did not have satisfactory documentary proof of her free status and was thus forced to hope that the city authorities would accept the testimony of a respectable and unimpeachable member of the community like Dereef.

4. Dereef could not relieve the woman because he was a free man of color. State law prohibited free men of color from being witnesses in any court, with the exception of a Magistrate's and Freeholders' Court trying a slave or free person of color for a criminal offense, in

which case the testimony would be without oath. Although the case of the woman who came to Dereef would be likely to appear before just such a court, Dereef's testimony could not be given under oath and, if the court was in the mood to enforce the letter of the law, the testimony would be worthless. O'Neall, *Negro Law of South Carolina*, 13.

5. In addition to the taxes assessed on all other residents of South Carolina, free persons of color were required to pay a state capitation tax. In 1860 the state capitation tax rate was $2.75 per adult. Free persons of color in Charleston were required to pay an additional capitation tax assessed by the city council. In 1860 a man between the ages of twenty-one and sixty "carrying on any trade, art, business, occupation, or employment, or being a mechanic within the city, or residing without the city, exercising his trade, art, business, occupation, or employment therein" was assessed ten dollars; males sixteen to twenty were taxed five dollars. Females from fourteen to seventeen paid a tax of three dollars; those between eighteen and fifty were taxed five dollars. The city did not neglect the collection of the capitation taxes because they were a valuable source of revenue.

For free persons of color, pay-

ing the capitation taxes was a heavy economic burden on top of all their other taxes. Yet payment of the capitation tax had been accepted for decades as de facto proof of free status. Being listed in the Charleston Free Negro Tax Books or possessing a receipt for the annual capitation tax had served many men and women of color as a sufficient indication of freedom. Legally, however, a free person of color could only prove his or her freedom by proving free birth (that is, that one was the child of a free mother) or that he or she had been freed before the legal prohibition of emancipation in 1820. Likewise, the provisions of the 1822 law had to be fulfilled. In the eyes of the law, a person who could not pass these tests was illegally living as a free person of color. William Ellison's daughter Maria was in precisely this situation (see note 1, above). O'Neall, *Negro Law of South Carolina*, 14; "A Bill to Raise Supplies for the Year One Thousand Eight Hundred and Sixty and Other Purposes," Charleston *Mercury*, March 14, 1860.

6. Slaves who worked for hire in Charleston were required by city law to wear badges that were purchased annually by their owners. In 1860 badges for "handicraft tradesmen" cost seven dollars each;

those for sellers of fruits, cakes, or other articles were five dollars; those for carters, draymen, fishermen, porters, and day laborers were four dollars; and those for fisherwomen, washerwomen, and house servants were two dollars. A badge was an official mark of slave status. A person who had been living as free and was enslaved lost all the legal protections of life and property that accrued to a free person of color: no property could be owned, no contracts made, no marriages solemnized, no law suits initiated, no assaults repelled. Over and above all these disabilities of slave status, any child of a woman who was thus enslaved would also become a slave for life. O'Neall, *Negro Law of South Carolina*; for examples of advertisements for slave badges, see Charleston *Mercury*, December 23, 1859, and January 21, 1860.

7. Free persons of color like the Ellisons, Johnsons, and Dereefs were exempt from legal challenges to their freedom under existing laws, as they could meet the required tests. However, every free person of color—including members of these elite families—was vulnerable to new laws which could impose drastic restrictions, require expulsion from the state, or even mandate enslavement. Such laws had been considered by the state legisla-

ture in 1859, as discussed above in the letters of December 23, 1859, and January 9, 1860. The crisis in Charleston convinced the Ellisons, Johnsons, and many others among the leading free colored families in Charleston and Stateburg that their exempt status would not last, as this and subsequent letters show.

8. The next regular session of the state legislature was to meet November 26, 1860.

9. Those who were being hunted down still had an opportunity to evade the police and leave the state. An amendment to the state law could foreclose the possibility of leaving.

10. The steamer *Keystone State* left Charleston for Philadelphia every ten days. A cabin ticket cost fifteen dollars; for another dollar one could go on to New York. Steerage to Philadelphia was six dollars. Advertisements for the *Keystone State* and other steamers appeared regularly in the Charleston newspapers.

11. Johnson was referring to *white* friends and counselors.

12. Whites.

13. Free persons of color.

14. In Charleston.

15. In other words, the white lawyer was convinced that the law prohibiting the return of free persons of color who had left the state would be strictly enforced.

16. Charleston slaveowners who did not annually purchase badges for their slaves were subject to heavy fines. The fine for a single failure to purchase a badge was twenty dollars. This suggests that the Dereefs paid fines for four slaves. According to the city tax list, Joseph Dereef owned six slaves and Richard E. Dereef owned fourteen. It is possible that the fine was assessed for the Dereefs' failure to buy badges for individuals they owned and used as slaves, either in their households or in their wood business. However, the context suggests that the individuals who had to take out badges had been living as free persons, although they were in fact legally owned by one of the Dereefs. The Dereefs may have owned these individuals outright and allowed them to live as free persons, or they may have held the individuals in trust, with conditions attached specifying that the individuals could live as free persons, under an arrangement similar to that between William Ellison and William McCreight for Ellison's daughter Maria (see note 1, above). The Dereefs also may have somehow permitted these individuals to claim them as their owners, in order to protect the individuals from being owned by public authorities or sold at auction. Whatever the specifics, the Dereefs' exemp-

tion from enslavement under the existing laws did not extend to an exemption from the closest scrutiny by the police. *List of the Taxpayers of Charleston, 1860*, 319; Walker, comp., *Ordinances of the City of Charleston*, 52.

17. John Lee was a member of the Brown Fellowship Society and the steward of the Charleston Club, a popular watering hole of the white aristocracy. According to the 1860 federal census, Lee was sixty-eight years old in 1860 and possessed real estate worth $6,000 and personal property valued at $100. Fitchett, "Free Negro in Charleston," 345; 1860 Population Schedules, Charleston, Ward 4, dwelling 243, SCDAH.

18. Samuel T. Demar, a free man of color, owned real property worth $2,000 and two slaves. One of them may have been his wife. Perhaps John Lee escorted Demar's wife to the steamer because Lee's standing in the eyes of whites was such that he would arouse less suspicion. According to an informant of E. Horace Fitchett, Lee always enjoyed an exemption from the law prohibiting travel outside the state because he had to travel extensively to procure supplies for the Charleston Club. *List of the Taxpayers of Charleston, 1859*, 387; *List of the Taxpayers of Charleston, 1860*, 319; Fitchett,

"Free Negro in Charleston,"
345–6.

19. There were several free men of color named Mathews in Charleston in 1860. However, Johnson was probably referring to the children of John B. Mathews, a fifty-year-old mulatto tailor. Mathews owned real estate worth $5,000 and personal property worth $600, including one slave, a woman about his age. She was probably his wife, which meant that his children were legally slaves—hence the urgency about getting them out of the city. Four free children were listed in Mathews's household in the 1860 federal census taken June 6, 1860: Elizabeth, 24, a mantua maker, like her sister Matilda, 20; Harriet, 17, a tailoress; and a 13-year-old boy, C. Pinckney. *List of the Taxpayers of Charleston, 1860*, 326; 1860 Population Schedules, Charleston, Ward 7, dwelling 84.

20. Perhaps William Lee, a member of the Brown Fellowship Society who lived on Calhoun Street, west of King. However, it has not been possible to prove that William was the brother of John Lee. List of Members of the Brown Fellowship Society, RSSL; Ford, *Census of Charleston, 1861*, 52.

21. The white friends of the free people of color in Charleston tended to be well-established merchants, lawyers, and plant-

ers. They were the customers in the shops run by tailors like Johnson and other free men of color. Like the leading members of the free colored community, they often worshipped in one of the Episcopal churches. As reputable and well-placed men in the white community, they could use their influence to shield free men of color they knew to be trustworthy and respectable from some of the threats to which they were legally vulnerable. White men of this sort probably served as the guardians of many of the free persons of color in Charleston, although it is impossible to be certain because no record of guardianship has survived among the Charleston Clerk of Court records. In general terms, their view of free people of color was stated by C. G. Memminger in his speech in the 1859 legislature against the bill to expel or enslave all free persons of color. See letter of December 23, 1859, notes 10 and 11, above.

22. The political power of the white workingmen in Charleston was increasing. They had representatives on the city council and had succeeded in making the mayor, Charles Macbeth, more and more responsive to their concerns. The white workingmen had few social, religious, or economic ties to the free colored community.

They tended to worship in one of the Methodist, Baptist, Lutheran, or Catholic churches. They bought their clothes off a rack or out of a barrel, and they observed and enforced the rules of racial etiquette (dark-skinned men must take the street side of the walk, they must uncover in the presence of whites, only white women can wear veils, and so on), although by no means predictably or continuously.

Seldom the friends of free persons of color, white workingmen were often the enemies of slaves, with whom they were in direct and unfair economic competition, they argued. Their biggest complaint was slaves who hired out their own time. Such slaves participated in the local job market more or less as free agents, finding jobs, striking agreements about wages and hours, and often living on their own beyond the supervision of their masters, to whom they returned a major portion of their wages. City ordinances strictly prohibited this practice and closely regulated the procedures by which masters could legally hire out their slaves to work for somebody else.

Despite the laws, it was simply impractical for masters to arrange personally for the employment of each slave they wanted to hire out. Masters commonly considered the laws a nuisance and ignored them. Slaves who hired their own time were a fixture of the Charleston labor pool. White mechanics periodically protested and organized petition campaigns for the enforcement of existing laws. In 1858 they mounted an effort in the state legislature to prohibit all slave hiring of any sort. Masters stoutly and successfully defended their prerogatives to do as they wished with their slave property. But as the mechanics continued to press for the prohibition of all slave hiring in the 1859 legislature and before the Charleston city council early in 1860, losing again each time, they managed to convince the mayor to order the police to enforce the existing laws.

According to city ordinances, any slave who was legally hired out was required to have a badge (see note 16, above). No badge was required if a slave was directly employed by his or her master. When the police arrested a slave who was working out without a badge, the slave's master had to buy a badge and pay a fine. In 1860, the number of arrests of slaves for working out without badges rose from zero in January, February, and March, to 27 in April, 45 in May, 32 in June, 40 in July, and to the unprecedented level of 93 in August. The large number of arrests in August certainly included some individuals who had lived as free persons, such as the servants of the Dereefs (see note 16, above). Many more individuals who had lived as free persons were forced to take out badges because they could not legally prove their free status (see notes 5 and 6, above). In fact, the August enslavement crisis in Charleston was the direct outgrowth of the white mechanics' insistence on rigid enforcement of the law governing slave hiring and requiring slave badges.

Although no official records have survived which document the exact mechanism by which the free colored community became the targets of the effort to enforce the laws about slave hiring, the procedure probably worked something like this: When the police dragnet picked up a dark-skinned man for a violation of the badge law and hauled him before the Mayor's Court, which heard such cases, the man might plead that he was in fact free and thus the law did not apply to him. Before August 1860, it is likely that if the man had paid the capitation tax as a free man of color and if he was so listed in the Free Negro Tax Book, his plea of free status would be accepted and he would be released. During the spring and summer crackdown of 1860, the mayor must have heard this plea many times. At some point, Macbeth—who was a lawyer—searched out the precise legal requirements for proof of free status and early in August he began to apply the tests required by the laws of 1820 and 1822. When he found that a large fraction of those individuals whose pleas of free status were supported by payment of the capitation tax and entry in the Free Negro Tax Book could not provide satisfactory legal proof of their freedom, he probably concluded that a correspondingly large proportion of the entire free colored community was in fact composed of individuals who were legally slaves, and thus in violation of the city badge law. He then ordered the police to take the appropriate steps. Evidence that this was how things worked comes from the only public notice in Charleston of the entire enslavement crisis. It appeared in the *Courier*, August 9, 1860, shortly after James M. Johnson had returned to Stateburg, and it is worth quoting in its entirety:

Sale of Badges—It is estimated that in the last two or three days as many as three or four hundred badges have been sold by the City Treasurer. Some sixty or seventy negroes have been brought up by the Police before the Mayor for working out without a badge. Most of them were those who were under a mistaken notion that they were free and did not require it. The law of 1822, however, forbids the emancipation in this State of any slave after that year. Many owners have liberated their slaves since 1822, without, perhaps, taking this law into consideration. Their slaves must have at least an owner in trust. The announcement by the Mayor that such negroes were not free, created considerable commotion among those outside who were similarly situated as the parties arrested—The rush to the Treasurer's office for badges, has, in consequence, been unusually large.

The prohibition of emancipation was in 1820, not 1822; see note 1, above.

23. The "higher class."

24. Persons who had been "lately freed" had the weakest cases, since exceptions to the 1820 prohibition on manumission could only be granted by specific acts of the state legislature. The many hundred other cases to which Johnson referred may have been less clear-cut, like the woman mentioned at the beginning of the letter who appealed to Joseph Dereef—she was in fact legally free, but she could not document her legitimate legal status (see notes 3 and 4, above). No record of any of these law suits has survived; neither the records of the Mayor's Court nor the Magistrate's and Freeholders' Court in Charleston are extant. The records of the Court of General Sessions, to which cases from the Magistrate's and Freeholders' Court could be appealed, contain a gap between 1840 and 1865. We are indebted to Marion Chandler of the South Carolina Department of Archives and History for advice and information about these records.

25. Although free persons of color were scattered throughout the city, there were important geographical gradients in their distribution. Few free persons of color lived in the aristocratic neighborhoods south of Broad Street. A majority (61 percent) of the free colored population in 1861 lived north of Calhoun Street. But Coming Street was the heart of the free colored community in the city. It contained 273 free persons of color in 1861, more than any other street in the city; Calhoun Street, the next most heavily populated by free persons of color, contained 185. Free persons of color composed 18 percent of the entire population of Coming Street (including slaves). They occupied 23 percent of the dwellings on the

street. Of the ten other streets in
the city that contained a total
population of 1,000 or more,
only two (Calhoun and St.
Philip) had as much as half the
proportion of free persons of
color as on Coming; all the rest
had between a third and a ninth
as many. In addition, some of
the most prominent members of
the free colored community
lived on Coming, including
William McKinlay, Jacob
Weston, and Mrs. Jeanette
Bonneau. That the police did
not visit Coming Street right
away probably reflected their
judgment that they would pick
up relatively few violations of
the badge law among its free
colored residents. One of the
reasons the Dereefs had already
been called upon may well have
been that they lived in the
northeast section of the city,
near the homes and workshops
of two of the leaders of the
white working men, James M.
Eason and Henry T. Peake (on
Eason and Peake, see letter of
December 7, 1860, note 7, below). Ford, *Census of the City of
Charleston, 1861*, 9, 15–20,
68–73.

26. Albert Aspinall was a
fifty-year-old tailor and a modest
property holder in the free colored community, reporting
$1,500 in real estate in the
1860 federal census. His partner was evidently Anthony
Plumet, a fifty-six-year-old free

mulatto tailor who lived next
door to Joseph Dereef on Amherst Street. Johnson's point
was that the man's freedom was
vulnerable to legal challenge.
That was probably why Plumet
did not pay any city taxes, although his wife Elizabeth paid
taxes on real estate valued at
$2,000. 1860 Population
Schedules, Charleston, Ward 5,
dwelling 179; and 1850 Population Schedules, Charleston
Neck, dwelling 672, SCDAH;
Ford, *Census of Charleston,
1861*, 32; *List of the Taxpayers
of Charleston, 1860*, 329.

27. Joseph Dereef.

28. Johnson was perhaps referring to the tailor shop of
Samuel Weston and Jacob
Weston at 128 Queen. Exactly
what "comfort" they could have
offered Aspinall's partner is not
clear. Perhaps Johnson's reference to Queen Street indicated
that the man would seek the advice and protection of an attorney on Queen. Ford, *Census of
Charleston, 1861*, 173.

29. Johnson was referring to
what he heard on his recent
train trip from Stateburg to
Charleston.

30. Members of the state legislature whose districts were
outside Charleston.

31. Free persons of color.

32. Free persons of color.

33. Free persons of color.

34. John Veree was a free
mulatto tailor who was a few

years older than James M. Johnson. Veree did not pay any city property taxes in 1859 or 1860. He lived at 6 Pitt Street, about a block from Johnson's residence on Coming. 1850 Population Schedules, Charleston, Ward 4, dwelling 575, SCDAH; Ford, *Census of Charleston, 1861*, 165.

35. Johnson's point was that the enslavement crisis in Charleston was not simply a local phenomenon; it was based on state law and could happen elsewhere in the state.

36. The reason the captain of the steamer put the white colored woman and her children ashore is unclear. Perhaps he feared that she or one of her children was a slave, in which case he would be guilty of aiding a slave to run away, a capital offense in South Carolina.

37. On July 3, two white men, Warren W. Andrews and Robert C. Browne, had a shoot-out in the streets of Charleston. As Andrews was riding past the Planters Hotel on Queen Street, Browne stepped out and began to fire on him. Andrews returned the fire. Browne was wounded in the knee and Andrews in the arm. But a stray bullet from one of the guns killed a thirty-five-year-old free colored carpenter, John Bennett. According to evidence presented to the hearing before the Jury of Inquest on Bennett's death, Browne's weapon

had fired seven shots, Andrews's three. Although Andrews's attorney argued that the bullet which killed Bennett was identical to the one that wounded Andrews and could not possibly have been fired from the gun used by Andrews, the judge concluded that it was impossible to be certain which weapon had killed Bennett. Curiously, while Browne was evidently never charged with any responsibility for Bennett's death, Andrews was indicted for murder by the Grand Jury and scheduled for trial in late January or early February 1861. For reasons that are not clear, the trial apparently never occurred. No mention of its disposal ever appeared in the detailed court reports published in the *Courier*, nor was Andrews among those sentenced for felonies in the 1861 session. Presumably, the charges against Andrews were dropped at the last minute. Johnson's statement that Browne was "awfully mortified" probably referred to Browne's leg, which may have become gangrenous. Less likely, Johnson's statement may have referred to Browne's humiliation and chagrin that another man was going to be tried for a murder that Browne himself had committed. Charleston *Courier*, July 6, 9, 1860; January 16, 17, and February 14, 15, 16, 1861.

38. Isham Moore was a

twenty-nine-year-old white planter from Sumter District who in 1860 owned real estate worth $15,000 and personal property valued at $30,000. 1860 Population Schedules, Sumter, dwelling 1042, SCDAH.

39. Summerville was a small town about 20 miles northwest of Charleston on the road to Columbia. Many residents of Charleston retreated there during the months of August and September, when the city was prone to deadly contagious diseases, especially yellow fever.

40. Mary M. Dereef was the daughter of Joseph Dereef. Her residence at Anderson Court House was recorded in the Charleston Free Negro Tax Book, 1862, CLS.

41. The town of Anderson was in the northwest corner of the state, over 200 miles from Charleston. Anderson could be reached by taking the South Carolina Railroad from Charleston to Columbia and the Greenville and Columbia Railroad on to Anderson.

42. Abigail Dereef was the nineteen-year-old daughter of Joseph Dereef. According to the 1860 federal census, she worked as a washerwoman. 1860 Population Schedules, Charleston, Ward 7, dwelling 219, SCDAH.

43. Perhaps Nelson Anderson, a thirty-five-year-old free colored porter. He paid no city property taxes and reported no wealth to the federal census enumerator. 1860 Population Schedules, Charleston, Ward 5, dwelling 213, SCDAH.

44. Jessie M. Dereef was the seventeen-year-old daughter of Joseph Dereef. 1850 Population Schedules, Charleston Neck, dwelling 673, SCDAH; Charleston Free Negro Tax Book, 1862, CLS.

45. James D. Johnson had left Charleston for Canada. James M. Johnson was probably referring here to an incident that occurred when his father arrived in Boston.

46. Probably Henry Lee, a free man of color who lived on Coming Street a few doors north of James D. Johnson. Ford, *Census of Charleston, 1861*, 68.

47. The famous Grand Trunk Railroad ran from Portland, Maine, to Montreal. Taylor and Neu, *The American Railroad Network*, 11.

48. Probably either Ann or Rebecca Merrill, two free women of color who lived in the same household in 1860 and were presumably sisters. They were thirty-one and forty-one years old, respectively. Neither paid any city property taxes or reported any wealth in the federal census. 1860 Population Schedules, Charleston, Ward 4, dwelling 853.

Charles Macbeth, 1873
From an original in the South Carolina Historical Society.
Photograph by Harold H. Norvell.

Charleston Aug 28th 1860

Dear Henry,

Yours is recd. I am sorry to hear of Wm[1] & Charlotte's[2] indisposition. We are not very well. The heat is oppressive.

The stir has subsided, but arrests are still made & the people are leaving.[3] It is vain for us to hope that if it is not the *will* of God he will not permit it. The bible tells us He is not the minister of Sin, & again the wicked shall flourish &c. In that model prayer we are taught to pray that His will may be done on earth as it is in heaven, & yet as free agents we are free to obey or reject. Hence it is that on earth wicked rule prevails, while in Heaven His will is done by the Just. I have implicit Faith in Providence & recognize its doing in directing those who seek His guidance, by overruling what is a present calamity to the future good of the virtuous. But I very much doubt that He wills or sanctions unrighteous acts, although in answer to prayer He often overthrows them & converts them into an engine of good provided we will act in accordance with His will as suggested by His Spirit & not supinely wait for the working of a miracle by having a Chariot let down to convey us away.

The magistrates boast of the good it has done them & Trusted that they did not know they were so rich.[4] Slaves have come by magic. It is evident that the movement is intended for their emolument. On the other hand it must prove the Death of many & the loss of earthly goods, the hard earnings of a life time, to others.[5] And yet those who put their trust in God may derive benefits spiritually & temporally.

Our Friends sympathise & express indignation which has checked it, but they are not in power & cant put down the majority.[6] Nothing more is heard of the suits.[7] Fordham[8] had to comply with the Law. Gen. Schnierlie[9] placed himself in the stead of a Man he holds & defied them to touch him. He would beat the one to Death who did. And Col. Whaley[10] says he will stand a lawsuit before complying, but the majority has succumbed.[11] The money has to come out of the purses of those held in Trust.[12]

Hicks[13] had his watch & chain taken from him in a Mob raised in Market St.

Col. Seymour[14] stood in front of our House speaking to an Irish carter on the subject & pointed to No 7 & 9[15] as being for sale. And you can see Hand bills on property held by cold. people in every quarter, which will have the effect of depreciation. The action of the people[16] has taken them by surprise & the originators[17] blame the Mayor for being so rash. They[18] say All[19] must leave but they did not want them ran off thus.

As it regards the Miss D's[20] I expected you to select for yourself first, which would be a good recommendation. They wont leave before their Father except entrusted to better hands. He is not disposed to move quick enough for them.

Father has been to Niagara Falls with Charley & to Love Feast & class meetings with Marshall[21] & R. Clark[22] & to pic nics with Gabriella & Charlotte[23] & is enjoying the sights with a zest. Charley begs to join with Father in Love to you & to assure you that you have never been forgotten.

Jas Glover[24] was taken to the Guard House at the instance of Dr Dessausure[25] for standing in a Drug store with his Hat on. I have not heard the sentence.[26] Beard[27] has closed his school & is about to leave before he is pounced upon.

Dr Dereef[28] is flourishing in Washington yet. He has written about 30 Letters home since he left. They come daily. If the one I saw is a sample he must have more constant employment than the Secry of State.

I cant write your Father for the present. I suppose the H & G affair[29] has attained the result. I fancy I see them in a Fond embrace.

W. P. Dacoster[30] appears to be circumspect. De Large[31] has got back to fret a few. Sasportas[32] has Returned from Aiken[33] with his daughter. They tried to prevail on him to make his abode there. The Family joins me in Love.

Yours,
J M J

1. William Ellison, Jr.

2. Charlotte was one of William Ellison, Sr.'s slaves. See the letter from William Ellison, Jr., March 26, 1857, note 16, above.

3. Arrests for the violation of the slave badge law were still being made and free persons of color were still leaving the state, although the extreme panic of the previous three weeks had subsided as the mayor responded to the criticism that he had acted precipitately. See note 17, below.

4. According to a state law of

1800, any slave who was emancipated illegally could be seized and made the property of any white person, on the grounds that the slave was abandoned property. The members of the Charleston free colored community who had to take out badges as slaves during the August enslavement crisis were in violation of both the municipal badge ordinance and the state law of 1820 prohibiting manumission. The city case was heard by the Mayor's Court, as was the state case; in the city the Mayor's Court substituted for the Magistrate's and Free-holders' Court, the lowest level of the state judicial system. The Magistrate's Court dealt exclusively with cases involving slaves and free persons of color. In noncapital cases such as illegal emancipation it included two magistrates and three free-holders or slaveholders. Conviction required the concurrence of two freeholders and the presiding magistrate. Free persons of color who had to take out city badges because they were unable to prove that they had not been illegally emancipated were required, of course, to have masters. If an individual did not have a master of record or a person who was willing to make a legal claim to be the individual's master—as was undoubtedly true of many of those who had to take out badges—then the individual was technically abandoned property and subject to seizure and ownership by any white person. In the enslavement crisis, such individuals were claimed by the mayor, Charles Macbeth, for the city, according to Johnson's statement in the letter. Legally, the city could have owned the slaves outright or sold them at public auction and split the proceeds with the state. McCord, *Statutes at Large*, vol. 7, 440–43; O'Neall, *Negro Law of South Carolina*, 9–15, 33–35.

5. Slaves were prohibited by state law from owning any property, real or personal. A master might allow a slave to have some personal belongings or a small amount of money, but legally it all belonged to the master. What happened to the property of those who had to take out badges during the enslavement crisis is not clear. It may have been claimed by the magistrates as abandoned property just like the newly enslaved individuals who had previously owned it. Or it may have been seized by the authorities for sale to the general public. Evidence in this and subsequent letters supports the latter possibility. O'Neall, *Negro Law of South Carolina*, 21.

6. White workingmen led the attack on the free people of color (see letter of August 20, 1860, note 22, above), but the aristocratic white "friends" of the free people of color still had their share of seats on the city council, representatives to the state legislature, and appointments to other public offices.

7. The lawsuits filed by free persons of color contesting the claim that they were legally slaves. See letter of August 20, 1860, note 24, above.

8. William Fordham, a thirty-five-year-old free man of color, was a barber. Evidently Fordham had to take out a badge as a slave. He appeared in the 1860 federal census as a free person of color, but not in the 1862 Free Negro Tax Book,

where his wife and children did appear. 1860 Population Schedules, Charleston, Ward 5, dwelling 122, SCDAH.

9. John Schnierle was a wealthy white man, the president of the local gas company, a major general in the South Carolina militia, and former mayor of Charleston. Schnierle owned real estate worth $26,400 and personal property worth $10,000, including the nineteen slaves on whom he paid city taxes in 1860. Schnierle lived at 21 Pitt Street, near Johnson's residence on Coming. According to Johnson's statement in the letter, Schnierle was the legal owner of a slave man he allowed to live as a free person of color. He probably held the man in a trust similar to that under which William Ellison, Sr. sold his daughter Maria to William McCreight. Schnierle defied the police to arrest him, since he was the legal owner of a slave who was living as a free man. He threatened to beat to death any policeman who arrested the man he held. 1860 Population Schedules, Charleston, Ward 4, dwelling 796, SCDAH; Ferslew, *Directory of Charleston, 1860*, 124; *List of the Taxpayers of Charleston, 1860*, 253.

10. William Whaley was a wealthy white attorney who lived south of Broad on Tradd Street. In 1860 he paid municipal taxes on 16 slaves and real

estate valued at $18,000. The lawsuit Whaley was willing to stand would probably have dealt with the question of whether Whaley could be forced to violate the terms of the trust he had (apparently) entered into; that is, to allow de facto freedom to a man who could not legally be freed because of the state prohibition on emancipation. Ferslew, *City Directory of Charleston, 1860*, 140; *List of the Taxpayers of Charleston, 1860*, 297.

11. Unlike Schnierle and Whaley, most of the white friends and guardians of free persons of color failed to come to their defense.

12. The individuals who had enjoyed de facto freedom while legally held in trust now had to pay for the slave badges they were required to take out. Perhaps they even had to pay the fines levied against their legal owners for neglecting to buy badges for them.

13. James Hicks was a free man of color about fifty years old who was a nurse. His well-dressed appearance perhaps outraged a group of whites in Market Street, the location of the large public markets. The apparel of slaves and free persons of color had been one of the complaints of the opponents of Mayor Charles Macbeth in his successful bid for reelection in the fall of 1859. Samuel Lord,

Jr., in a speech for Macbeth's opponent, John E. Carew, echoed sentiments expressed by several others when he said, "We object to the unbridled license and immunities afforded the colored population of our city, breaking down the lines of due subordination and respect between the slave and master. . . ." A watch and chain on the person of a free man of color could be considered evidence of insubordination and justification for the white mob to attack Hicks. During the mayoral campaign, "Another Voter" had urged a "return to the 'good-old-times' when these ebon dames neither preserved their complexions from a darker shade, by wearing 'uglies' and veils, nor swept the sidewalks with their rich brocades and silks, and when the dandy barber and tailor-boy did not sport his 'puppy switch' or perfume the air with his fragrant weed." A letter from "A Resident and Native" put the question even more pointedly: "Shall they [slaves and free Negroes], in silks and laces, promenade our principal thoroughfares, with the arrogance of equals—by their insolent bearing making the modest lady yield them the walk, and the poor white woman to feel that to be virtuous and honest gives her place, in appearances, below the slaves, in the gratification of her desire for dress and distinction?" Charleston Free Negro Tax Book, 1862, CLS; Charleston *Mercury*, October 21, 25, 26, 27 and November 1, 1859; Charleston *Courier*, October 26, 1859.

14. Robert W. Seymour was a prosperous white attorney who lived on Franklin Street, a few blocks south of Coming. In 1860 Seymour paid city taxes on 16 slaves and real estate of his own valued at $10,000 and other real estate of which he was trustee valued at $68,400. In the 1859 mayoral election Seymour had supported Macbeth's reelection, arguing that the mayor insisted on "rigid and strict enforcement of the laws; [and] that he knew no distinction of persons." 1860 Population Schedules, Charleston, Ward 4, dwelling 454, SCDAH; Ferslew, *City Directory of Charleston, 1860*, 125; *List of the Taxpayers of Charleston, 1860*, 256; Charleston *Mercury*, October 27, 1859.

15. James D. Johnson had put his houses on the market before he left for Canada. (See letter of September 3, 1860, below.) Since Johnson had left Charleston before the enslavement crisis occurred, that could not have influenced his decision to sell. More likely he intended to use the proceeds from his houses to finance his declining years. He was sixty-seven in 1860. His trip to Canada and

the attempt to sell his houses evidently reflected his decision to retire from his work as a tailor.

16. The actions of the free persons of color in selling off their property and leaving the state surprised the white community.

17. In other words, the leaders of the white workingmen who had urged the mayor to enforce the law now blamed him for the unexpected consequences of his compliance with their wishes. By moving so precipitately against free people of color, the mayor had succeeded in raising the issues of justice and equity. Rather than congratulating the mayor, some whites extended their sympathies to free Negroes. Thus, rather than solving the problem, Macbeth had engendered an unexpected white backlash against such drastic measures.

18. The originators, the leaders of the white workingmen.

19. All free persons of color.

20. The daughters of Joseph Dereef, whom Johnson had mentioned in his previous letter to Henry; see letter of August 20, 1860, notes 40, 42, 44, above.

21. Johnson was evidently referring to a person named Marshall Clark. However, no free man of color with this name or with the surname Marshall appeared in the 1861 Canadian census of Toronto. Nonetheless,

Marshall may have been a relative of R. Clark (see note 22, below) and thus been a free man of color from Charleston. Canada West Census, 1861, Toronto, Reels 172–180, PA.

22. Although no free man of color named R. Clark appeared in the 1861 Canadian census of Toronto, Richard Clark, William Clark, and Francis Clark were listed in the Charleston Free Negro Tax Books in 1849 and 1850, but not subsequently. According to fragments of a letter and a contemporary newspaper clipping, Richard Holloway Clark, whose grandmother was evidently Elizabeth Holloway of Charleston, was a trader in Toronto who, twelve months after arriving in the city in 1856, declared bankruptcy. Thus the R. Clark to whom Johnson was referring was probably a free man of color from Charleston who was currently living in Canada. Charleston Free Negro Tax Books, 1849, 1850, SCDAH; Canada West Census, 1861, Toronto, Reels 172–180, PA; R. C. Clark to My Beloved Grandmother, December 1, 1856, and clipping, October 30, 1856, Holloway Scrapbook, RSSL.

23. Charley's daughter, who lived with him and Gabriella in Toronto. Canada West Census, 1861, Toronto, St. John's Ward, District 3, Reel 178, folio 598, PA.

24. James Glover was a

young free man of color who worked on the railroad. Charleston Free Negro Tax Book, 1862, CLS.

25. Henry W. DeSaussure was a prosperous white physician in his mid-forties. In 1860 he paid municipal taxes on 14 slaves and real estate worth $8,000. His office was on Meeting Street, near the Mills House. 1860 Population Schedules, Charleston, Ward 4, dwelling 451, SCDAH; Ferslew, *Directory of Charleston, 1860*, 60; *List of the Taxpayers of Charleston, 1860*, 25.

26. DeSaussure considered Glover's failure to remove his hat an act of insolence, which legally was tantamount to an assault. DeSaussure would have been within his rights if he had personally attacked Glover. By having Glover taken to the Guard House, DeSaussure insured that the case would be heard before the Mayor's Court. The sentence for insolence could include whipping and imprisonment. In June, for example, a case of insolence on the part of a free man of color was punished by thirteen paddles and ten days in jail. O'Neall, *Negro Law of South Carolina*, 13; Charleston *Courier*, June 28, 1860.

27. Edward Beard was a nineteen-year-old free man of color, a bricklayer, who ran a school for free colored children on Coming Street, according to

C. W. Birnie. He lived with his three brothers—two of whom were tailors—his sister, and his mother at 105 Coming. An 1834 state law prohibited any free person of color from running a school for slaves or free Negroes on pain of fine, imprisonment, and corporal punishment. In addition, Beard's own freedom may not have been exempt from legal challenge under the laws of 1820 and 1822. The children who attended Beard's school and others like it had certainly not escaped public notice. During the 1859 mayoral campaign, "A Slaveholder" had complained "of the many evils which are secretly undermining our institutions" and headed his list with "the crowds of black children who throng our streets every morning on their way to school, with satchel well filled with books." None of the Beards appeared in the 1862 Free Negro Tax Book. Birnie, "Education of the Negro in Charleston," 19; O'Neall, *Negro Law of South Carolina*, 23; McCord, *Statutes at Large*, 468; 1860 Population Schedules, Charleston, Ward 8, dwelling 46, SCDAH; Ford, *Census of Charleston, 1861*, 69; Charleston *Mercury*, October 25, 1859.

28. Probably J. M. F. or J. R. E. Dereef, the sons of Richard E. Dereef, the wealthy wood factor. However, we have found no evidence that either of these young men was a doctor.

In the 1862 Free Negro Tax Book both men were listed as factors. Johnson may have been referring to some other Dereef who was a doctor or the title may have had a meaning other than the obvious.

29. Noah Graham had recently been installed as the ordinary of Sumter District; as such he was involved in the disposition of William Ellison's estate after his death in 1861. The character of Graham's dispute with Hennegan is unknown, but Johnson mentioned it again and identified the principals in the letter of September 3, 1860, note 47, below. William Ellison Estate Papers, Box 151, Package 8, Sumter County Estate Papers, SCDAH; Charleston *Mercury*, February 20, 1860.

30. Dacoster was the machinist who had a drinking problem. See letters of April 28, 1860, note 5 and May 5, 1860, note 8, above.

31. John DeLarge was a forty-year-old free mulatto tailor and steward. Like Johnson, DeLarge lived on Coming Street and worshipped at Grace Episcopal Church. In 1860, DeLarge paid municipal tax on real estate valued at $2,000. 1860 Population Schedules, Charleston, Ward 6, dwelling 73, SCDAH; *List of the Taxpayers of Charleston, 1860*, 318; Ford, *Census of Charleston, 1861*, 72; Parish Register, Grace Episcopal Church, Charleston.

32. Probably Frederick Sasportas, the free colored millwright; see the letter of May 14, 1860, note 14, above.

33. Aiken was a small town about 125 miles northwest of Charleston, about 15 miles from the Savannah River and Augusta, Georgia. A branch of the South Carolina Railroad ran between Charleston and Augusta, through Aiken.

Charleston, Septr 3d, 1860

Dear Henry,

Your favor of 2 inst is recd. I am glad to hear of the good health of the Stateburgians with a few exceptions. Vague Rumors have been afloat for several days prejudicial to the health of the City & is now confirmed by the papers reporting one or two fatal cases of Fever.[1] The weather at present is favorable to its spread. I will await further developments and trust in Providence, hoping at the same time the news may not reach E. Ann, as in that event I would have to leave to allay her anxiety. I am not apprehensive & the best course for me to pursue would be to remain at my post, as there would be more danger in my return after leaving. I shall not hint to E. Ann & hope she may [*not*] have her fear aroused. I have heard of 10 cases last week in a certain locality. They were said to be Typhoid & Billious but I had my suspicions.

Messers Anthony & Saml Weston[2] called on Mayor McBeth to get him to certify to the falsity of a Report that one of the Miss Westons had undergone punishment for insolence to a Lady. It was corrected in the Courier of the 1st inst & they admitted to be Respectable & their families of respectability.[3] It originated from the case of Louisa Thompson[4] who was sentenced to 5 paddles & days imprisonment for striking against a Lady. Her Brother[5] appeared & claimed White Laws.[6] The paddles were omitted & the imprisonment imposed & by the way of balancing the acct her Brother was ferreted out at his House & beat by Police Officers for presuming to say she was as white as those who arrested [*her*]. He made complaint to the chief[7] who took the officers aside & sent him home. He may look to be redressed with another Walloping. From such peace officers we may well seek deliverance.

Glover[8] was let off with a Fine of $5. His guardian,[9] as an excuse for his rushing into a drug store with his hat on, [*said*] That any servant would be in a hurry when he has a distance to go & it was late & he without a pass.[10] This saved his paddles.

Billy's bro in law,[11] who has a wife at Adger's,[12] had some difficulties with a servt in the yard & the police took him out & at the same sitting of the Court [*he*] was sentenced to a paddling, which gave Dr Geddings[13] the Job of putting a plaster on his posterior. The Dr said it should have been settled by their owners, the police had nothing to do with it.[14] Adger was absent & the man's master [*did not*] expect his servt to be dealt with so. The Mayor is getting a reputation.

There was a case Reported by Moses Levy[15] of a F. M. C. returning by Steamer,[16] with the Remarks that Off. L.[17] would put a stop to the practice, it was too common with females especially. Several were seen promenading on Broadway & then they would return here as coolly as whites.[18] It proved to be [J] Noisette[19] who left a month ago to elude his creditors, sold out his furniture &c & left his wife who has since had a child, to carry out the child's play. After pleading with Ryan[20] to get him off on the Steamer & only being allowed by Mr Adger[21] interceding, as the Captn said the penalty was $1000,[22] he foolishly secreted himself[23] & when the Captn found it out, he got so vexed he confined him and handed him over to Levy on arrival. The Mayor turned over the case to a Magistrate & Ryan who sent him got Campbell[24] to clear by plea of being a Servant.[25] He is now hiding from his creditors.

Frs Smith[26] is just from Queen St. & tells me that Mr S. W.[27] went alone. His daughter[28] had a bad hand & was down at the Island[29] & was asked if the whipping did her so. It was getting credence among the whites & he thought it best to stop. A & S[30] were both named in the papers, as Report included both. The Mayor said he must break the first fellow's head that said so.

Thos Webb Esqr[31] told a man who was beat by the same offr at Thompsons,[32] in his the offr presence, to take a stick & beat the first fellow that entered his House & the Mayor too & he would take the consequences. Thompson had 2 gents[33] with him, but they were not of the Webb stamp. If there were a few more of the same sort, they[34] would get their deserts. The Offr gave the man 25 cts to get a [court] plaster for his wounds. Webb Rallied him on that.

Noisette's adviser was J L. Francis[35] so far as eluding creditors went. He carried out his practice in concealing himself.

The tide of emigration has not stopped. The accounts from those who have left thus far are encouraging.

Bing[36] has an addition to the Family in the Shape of a Foundling at his door when his [*four illegible words*] have an even dozen in Family. He has some [*one or two illegible words*] "*Hennegan & Graham*"[37] have they got together. I alluded to that. Father is awaiting H R Harrarals.[38] Mother & Margaret Joins me in Love as Ever,

Yrs Truly

J M Johnson

P. S. Positive Sale. No 7 & 9[39] has been up for Sale before Father left. It goes to the highest bidder. Judge Magrath[40] had me in chambers yesterday. He is to give advance & then the work will be started Septr 4th.

1. In August and September, Charleston was subject to yellow fever epidemics. In 1858 the disease had killed hundreds. Individuals who had recently arrived in the city were especially susceptible to the disease, caused by a virus transmitted by the bite of a female mosquito that bred in pools of stagnant water, of which Charleston had all too many.

2. The brothers Anthony and Samuel Weston were leaders in the free colored community in Charleston. Anthony Weston was a seventy-year-old millwright who lived on Calhoun Street. In the 1860 federal census, he reported owning real estate valued at $5,000 and personal property worth $8,000. His wife Maria paid municipal taxes on 14 slaves and real estate valued at $40,075. Together, they were easily the wealthiest free colored family in Charleston. Samuel Weston was a sixty-year-old tailor, who had a shop on Queen Street with his brother Jacob Weston and a home on Mazyck Street. Samuel paid municipal taxes on one slave of his own, ten slaves he held in trust, and real estate valued at $9,300. His wife Harriet also paid taxes on a slave and $3,000 worth of real estate. Both Samuel and Anthony Weston had daughters who were in their twenties. It would have taken nerves of steel for ei-

ther of the Westons to call on the mayor to protest the rumor; both of them had been freed *after* the 1820 prohibition on manumission. They officially received their freedom in 1833 by the provisions of the will of their owner, the wealthy rice planter Plowden Weston. 1860 Population Schedules, Charleston, Ward 4, dwelling 161, Ward 5, dwelling 137, SCDAH; Ford, *Census of Charleston, 1861*, 51, 151, 173; *List of the Taxpayers of Charleston, 1860*, 332; Will of Plowden Weston, *Charleston Wills*, vol. 37, 165–85, CCL.

3. On September 1, 1860, the *Courier* printed the following notice on page two between notices for the Hillsboro Military Academy and the International Police Exchange:

It has been currently rumored that a female member of the family of either *Anthony* or *Samuel Weston* had offered some violence to a lady in the street. These *Westons* are very respectable colored persons and esteemed in the community for their character and deportment at all times. We have therefore enquired into the matter, and find that the rumor is entirely untrue and without foundation. [Italics in the original.]

4. Louisa Thompson was a free colored washerwoman about thirty years old who lived

on St. Philip Street. According to both the 1860 federal census and the city tax list, she was propertyless. 1860 Population Schedules, Charleston, Ward 6, dwelling 129, SCDAH.

5. William Thompson, Louisa's brother, was a twenty-year-old free mulatto laborer. Like Louisa, he too was propertyless. They lived in the same household on St. Philip Street along with five siblings, ages fourteen to three. 1850 Population Schedules, Charleston Neck, dwelling 320, and 1860 Population Schedules, Charleston, Ward 6, dwelling 129, SCDAH.

6. Legally, a free person of color was prohibited from striking a white person. In the words of John Belton O'Neall, one of the state's most distinguished jurists, "They cannot repel force by force; that is they cannot strike a white man, who may strike any of them." A claim to be covered by white laws was an attempt to circumvent this prohibition and make possible an argument that the assault on the white lady was justified. If the claim to be covered by white laws were sustained, it would also have many other legal implications. There was no firm legal definition of a white person. O'Neall advised that, "Whenever the African taint is so far removed, that upon inspection a party may be fairly pronounced to be white,

and such has been his or her previous reception into society, and enjoyment of the privileges usually enjoyed by white people, the Jury may rate and regard the party as white. . . . When the [Negro] blood is reduced to, or below ⅛, the Jury ought always to find the party *white*. When the blood is ¼ or more African, the Jury must find the party a mulatto." The decision in any particular case was always in the hands of a jury, which, despite the flexibility and ambiguity of the law, tended to adopt the one-drop rule. Thus in Charleston and elsewhere, individuals who were visibly white were socially and legally colored. (See for example Johnson's mention of a white colored lady in the letter of August 20, 1860, note 36, above.) In the 1860 federal census, which was taken two months before the insolence incident, Louisa Thompson was listed as a "mulatto." About all that can be taken to mean, however, is that she was not visibly black. O'Neall, *Negro Law of South Carolina*, 6, 13.

7. H. L. Bass, a white man, was the captain of the city police force. Ferslew, *Directory of Charleston, 1860*, 39.

8. James Glover had been arrested for having his hat on in a drug store. See letter of August 28, 1860, notes 24, 25, and 26, above.

9. Glover's white guardian, as

required by the law of 1822. See letter of August 20, note 1, above.

10. Charleston observed a ten o'clock curfew during the spring and summer. Any slave or free person of color on the streets after that hour was subject to arrest by the city police, unless the person had a pass from his or her white master or employer, specifically stating that person had good reason to be out after curfew.

11. A slave.

12. Probably Robert Adger, a wealthy white merchant. Adger paid city taxes on seventeen slaves and real estate worth $30,400. His brother, the banker James Adger, paid city taxes on only one slave, although he owned real estate valued at $20,000. Another brother, Joseph Ellison Adger, the hardware merchant with whom William Ellison did business (see letter of March 26, 1857, note 12, above), owned only four slaves and real estate assessed at $12,000. Their father, the wharf owner James Adger, had recently died leaving an estate which included three slaves in the city and real estate valued at $101,500. In any case, one of the Adgers owned the wife of Billy's brother-in-law, who had a disagreement with one of the other slaves in Adger's slave yard. *List of the Taxpayers of Charleston, 1860*, 4.

13. Although there were two other physicians named Geddings in Charleston, this was probably Dr. Eli Geddings who lived on George Street. Dr. Geddings paid city taxes on sixteen slaves and $54,000 in real estate. *List of the Taxpayers of Charleston, 1860*, 102; Ford, *Census of Charleston, 1861*, 93.

14. That is, the disagreement between the two slaves—Billy's brother-in-law and a slave in Adger's yard—should have been resolved by their masters, not the police.

15. Moses Levy was an eighty-five-year-old white man who listed his occupation as "Gentleman." Levy lived south of Broad on Tradd Street, just opposite Adger's wharves, where New York steamers docked. Levy, one of many white Charlestonians born in Germany, was prosperous, but not wealthy; he reported to the federal census marshal real estate worth $12,000 and personal property worth $4,000. 1860 Population Schedules, Charleston, Ward 6, dwelling 32, SCDAH; Ford, *Census of Charleston, 1861*, 204.

16. Levy reported the case of a free man of color who illegally returned to Charleston on a steamer, after having left the state. For a description of the law, see the letter of August 4, 1860, note 2, above.

17. Edwin Levy, the son of Moses Levy, was a twenty-four-

year-old sergeant in the city police force. Sergeant Levy resided with his father, according to the listing in the 1860 federal census. Same sources as note 15, above.

18. In other words, Levy reported that several free women of color from Charleston who were seen promenading on Broadway in New York City had returned to Charleston in violation of the law prohibiting their reentry into South Carolina.

19. Joseph Noisette was the free man of color whose return by steamer Levy had reported. Noisette was a thirty-year-old farmer who owned real estate worth $8,000 and personal property worth $8,000, according to the 1860 federal census. Noisette lived on the north end of King Street, almost directly across the street from another residence of Moses Levy. 1860 Population Schedules, Charleston, Ward 7, dwelling 357, SCDAH; Ford, *Census of Charleston, 1861*, 117, 125.

20. There were a number of white men named Ryan in Charleston in 1860. The Ryan to whom Johnson was referring was in New York at the time Noisette pleaded with him, was known to Noisette, Johnson, and Henry Ellison, and apparently had some influence with the captain of the steamer, or at least was known to him and to Adger. It is possible that John-

son was referring to W. K. Ryan, a factor and commission merchant, whose offices were on Boyce and Company's Wharf, a short distance up the waterfront from Adger's wharves. W. K. Ryan lived on Thomas Street, several blocks north of Johnson's Coming Street residence and near many other free colored families. Ryan paid city taxes on six slaves and real estate valued at $6,000. Ford, *Census of Charleston, 1861*, 203, 226; *List of the Taxpayers of Charleston, 1860*, 248.

21. Probably James Adger, the son of the recently deceased wharfowner, whose offices were on Adger's North Wharf, as were the offices of the New York steamship line and of the factors with whom the Ellisons did business, Adams and Frost. See also note 12, above. Ford, *Census of Charleston, 1861*, 224.

22. The captain was well informed. If he were to be convicted of having brought a free person of color into the state in violation of the state law of 1835, he was subject to a fine of up to $1,000 and up to six months imprisonment. O'Neall, *Negro Law of South Carolina*, 15.

23. By hiding away aboard the steamer, Noisette made it appear as if he, and by implication, the captain, were involved in a surreptitious reentry into the state. By confining Noisette, the captain exculpated himself.

Apparently, he had expected Noisette to act normally aboard the steamer and brazen out his landing in Charleston. Because Noisette had been out of town for a month, he may not have known about the enslavement crisis in Charleston and the hypervigilant police. He may have been hiding simply to continue to evade his creditors. The captain, who traveled to Charleston every ten days, knew what was going on in the city.

24. James B. Campbell was a wealthy white attorney in Charleston, who lived on Beaufain Street, not far from Coming. Campbell reported real estate worth $20,000 and personal property valued at $60,000 to the federal census marshal, although he paid city taxes on only $3,000 in real estate and six slaves. Ryan arranged for Campbell to argue Noisette's case involving violations of state law. 1860 Population Schedules, Charleston, Ward 4, dwelling 897, SCDAH; *List of the Taxpayers of Charleston, 1860*, 45; Ford, *Census of Charleston, 1861*, 39.

25. In other words, the successful plea was that Noisette was on the trip to New York as the servant of a white man. In effect, he had a pass from his alleged employer to leave and return to the state. The success of such a plea before the court was probably dependent on Noisette's long residence in the city and on the community standing of Campbell and Ryan.

26. Francis Smith was a free colored tailor about fifty years old who lived on Henrietta Street. 1862 Free Negro Tax Book, CLS.

27. Samuel Weston went alone to see the mayor. See note 2, above.

28. Hannah Weston, Samuel Weston's daughter, was twenty-five years old. 1860 Population Schedules, Charleston, Ward 4, dwelling 161, SCDAH.

29. Sullivan's Island, fronting the Atlantic Ocean at the mouth of Charleston harbor, almost due east of the city, was a popular summertime retreat for Charlestonians. A ferry service connected the island and the city.

30. Anthony and Samuel Weston. See notes 2 and 3, above.

31. Thomas L. Webb was a factor and commission merchant whose offices were on North Commercial Wharf. Webb, who was white, lived on Cannon Street, just west of Coming. In 1860 he paid municipal taxes on $9,800 worth of real estate and four slaves. 1860 Population Schedules, Charleston, Ward 8, dwelling 64, SCDAH; Ford, *Census of Charleston, 1861*, 64, 228.

32. The incident involving William Thompson, described above. (See notes 4, 5, 6, and

7.) In other words, Webb told the free man of color to beat the first white man who entered his house, even if it was the mayor, and he (Webb) would take the consequences.

33. Two white men.

34. The police would get what they deserved, if there were a few more white men as courageous as Webb.

35. John L. Francis was a prosperous free mulatto barber. He paid city taxes on real estate worth $11,600 and seven slaves. His shop was in the same building as James D. Johnson's tailor shop on King Street. 1860 Population Schedules, Charleston, Ward 4, dwelling 252, SCDAH; *List of the Taxpayers of Charleston, 1860*, 321; Ford, *Census of Charleston, 1861*, 121.

36. John Bing was a free mulatto tailor, thirty-eight years old, whose household already included four children between the ages of thirteen and five, according to the 1860 federal census. Bing paid no city property taxes and, according to the federal census, was propertyless. The reference to "an even dozen" probably meant John Bing's father, the free colored carter Gordon Bing, who had twelve children at the time of the 1850 census. 1850 Population

Schedules, Charleston Neck, dwelling 381, and 1860 Population Schedules, Charleston, Ward 3, dwelling 291, SCDAH.

37. The dispute between these two Sumter men was referred to in the letter of August 28, 1860, note 31, above.

38. The Harrals were a white family who ran a saddlery and hardware shop on Meeting Street and lived at 4 Glebe, within two blocks of Johnson's house on Coming. Like Johnson, the Harrals had lived in Charleston for more than twenty years. Ferslew, *Directory of Charleston, 1860*, 76.

39. James D. Johnson's houses, 7 and 9 Coming Street.

40. A. G. Magrath was the judge in the federal court in Charleston. He lived on Calhoun, near Ashley. He did not pay municipal taxes in 1860 nor did he list any property, real or personal, in the 1860 federal census. Evidently, Magrath had called James M. Johnson into his chambers to take his measurements for some clothing Johnson was to begin on September 4, as soon as Magrath had paid an advance on the order. 1860 Population Schedules, Charleston, Ward 4, dwelling 822, SCDAH; Ferslew, *Directory of Charleston, 1860*, 97.

Charleston Septr 7th 1860

Dear Henry

Yours of 6th bearing the sad news of Poor Jane's Death[1] is recd. I was very much shocked although I told Mother of my apprehension for her safety when I returned. The Lord is long suffering & of tender mercy & I doubt not that those who are reared with imperfect conception of his attributes & devine government are the object of his condescending Love & Mercy. I trust that the deceased as one of those may be a recipient of that provision & her Soul be saved [*illegible word*]. It adds to the severity of the stroke that she is taken off in the morn of Life & without a moments warning. But it is the will of God & we dare not murmur. He doeth what seemeth good in his sight. I pray that it may have a salutary effect on us all & especially those who are closely allied to deceased & do not consider their latter end.[2] How vividly does this afflicting & sudden dispensation recall the exhortation I was listening to from Mark 13c 32v[3] at St. Lukes Wednesday morning while you were witnessing a [practical] case. Rev. Gadsden[4] [delivered] with much force on the necessity of Watchfulness & Prayer from the fact that we knew not the hour of his coming & it was spoken of in scripture as being sudden & unexpected. Dear Little Sis[5] I hope she may never feel the want of a Mother's care.

I would have been up on Thursday were it not for the Reports that got out & even after it was doubted would have come were it not that persons who have been absent only in the country & returned have been taken down with Typhoid & Broken bone Fever which is prevalent. I think the city is healthy if persons would not be excited & travel to & fro to agitate the Bile which originates in Billious & is apt to terminate in Typhoid. I have been regular in my habits & use precautions in my diet, so that my system is not susceptible to contagion & for the rest I trust in an All Wise Providence. Mother & Margaret[6] unite in sympathy with you to the Family at Wisdom & Drayton Hall. I am yrs truly,

J M Johnson

1. Jane Buckner, the wife of John Buckner, James M. Johnson's stepson. Jane may have been James M. Johnson's sister; see letter of September 16, note 5, below. On the marriage of John and Jane Buckner, see letter of March 26, 1857, note 15, above.

2. Apparently Johnson was referring to John Buckner. Although Buckner was married by the rector of Holy Cross Church and had his daughter

Harriet Ann baptized in the church June 22, 1860, there is no record of his having been baptized or confirmed. Record of the Claremont Parish, 1809–1866, Church of the Holy Cross, Stateburg, SCL.

3. "But of that day and *that* hour knoweth no man, no, not the angels which are in heaven, neither the Son, but the Father." The Authorized King James Version.

4. The rector of St. Luke's in Charleston; see letter of December 23, 1859, note 3, above.

5. Johnson was referring to Harriet Ann Buckner, the two-year-old daughter of John and Jane Buckner. She was born March 25, 1858. Same source as note 2, above.

6. Margaret was James M. Johnson's cousin; see letter of January 9, 1860, note 9, above.

Toronto Sept 16th 1860

My Dear Henry

I have been away from home now some five weeks and have not yet sent you the first note of my travel. Well sir here goes for it. I left Charleston on the 7th August for Boston arrived their on Tuesday and left the same afternoon for this place via "Portland" "Montreal" the "Victoria Bridge" to Kingston.¹ It is scarcely possible for me to give you an idea of all that I have seen since I left home.

The Victoria Bridge is of its kind the grandest structure in the world.² Then I visited the "Falls" the falls of Niaggara with its suspension bridge of its kind another grand piece of work.³ Then again I saw two men (on the same day whilst standing upon this same grand and I may add marvellous piece of work—the bridge) walk across the River Niaggara on a rope take a cooking stove on his back place it on the rope make a fire and then cook eggs.

I have seen many more things. I have seen the most magnificent buildings. I have seen all colors and classes obtain admission to them and I have seen people apparently happy but I have not seen much money. It seems a scarce article. I have seen this city lit up with gas representing all the varied forms which it were possible for the most fertile imagination to depict. I have [seen] the streets presenting the appearance of a flower garden. I have seen riches of the most magnificent description towering over the streets. I have seen the streets lined with thousands and tens of thousands, and have heard 5000 children sing "God save the Queen" and all this for the coming of the "prince of Wales"⁴ and I have seen the Prince the apparent heir to the Throne of England.

These are some of the things I have seen and yet I yearned for my home but only because I left their some of those and the one I most dearly loved and cared for, such is life dear Henry. I regret to learn through James that things looks so dark and gloomy at home. What will be the issue I fear to think. I am afraid that it will come to leaving.

This is to my mind a poor country but some persons are living in it. It is cool at present. I do not know that I can write you of many things which will interest you from this part. Every body is getting along, though by appearance slowly.

From recent news received from James I doubt the propriety of my return⁵ and this makes me feel the more anxious as for instance here I have your trunk. I cannot describe my feeling. I am really comfortable and yet from the pressure which may occur by a return I am miserable.

J F Mosiman[6] has taken this third wife, a large blustering looking English girl. Our folks are all well, sends their regards to you. Extend the same to your father, Brothers, Jno,[7] his wife & my daughter[8] & Believe me yours truly

J. D. Johnson

How do Henry my dear friend. The regards of *all* my family, Mrs Miller[9] & her family to you and yours. Your friend

Charley

1. Johnson traveled on the Grand Trunk Railroad from Portland, Maine, to Toronto.

2. The Victoria Bridge over the St. Lawrence River at Montreal was over a mile long. Built by Robert Stephenson, the famous British bridge builder, it was completed in 1859. Smith, *The World's Great Bridges*, 72. For an excellent illustration of the bridge, see Plowden, *Bridges: The Spans of North America*, 108–109.

3. The Niagara suspension bridge was the first successful railway suspension bridge in the world. Rail traffic was on the upper deck of the bridge, roadway traffic on the lower. The innovative American bridge builder John A. Roebling built the bridge, using cables composed of iron wires to suspend the span of over 800 feet some 245 feet above the rapids. Roebling completed the bridge in 1855. See Plowden, *Bridges*, 110–111 for a drawing of the bridge.

4. The Prince of Wales, Albert Edward (who became King Edward VII in 1901),

visited Canada in late August and early September. His reception could not have been more enthusiastic nor could newspapers have been more generous with their coverage of his ceremonial activities. See, for example, any issue of the Toronto *Daily Globe* from mid-August to late September.

5. The letter he had received from James M. Johnson made him fear that the South Carolina law prohibiting the reentry of free persons of color who had left the state would be enforced and he would not be allowed to return to Charleston. For discussion of the letter from James, see letter of September 24, 1860, below.

6. No free man of color by this name appeared in the 1861 Canadian census of Toronto. However, a free man of color named John F. Mosiman lived in Charleston in 1843, and in 1845 the rector of St. Philip's Episcopal Church in Charleston presided at his marriage to Anna Mishaw, who was probably the sister of William Ellison Jr.'s wife, Mary T. Mishaw.

Canada West Census, 1861, Toronto, Reels 172–180, PA; Charleston Free Negro Tax Book, 1843, SCDAH; Fitchett, "Free Negro in Charleston," 46.

7. John Buckner.

8. Apparently Johnson was referring to Buckner's wife Jane (who had recently died) as his daughter; see letter of September 7, 1860, note 1, above.

9. Although no free woman of color named Miller appeared in the 1861 Canadian census of Toronto, Charley may well have been referring to Gabriella's mother (his mother-in-law). According to a report published many years later in the Columbia, South Carolina, *State* (October 4, 1931), several members of Gabriella's family resided in Canada. Source of Canadian census same as in note 6, above.

Charleston Sept 24 1860

Dear Henry

Yours of 23d enclosing Father's favor is recd. I am obliged to you for forwarding it. The letter that gave the unpleasant news was for Charley & sent by Mr Oakes[1] during the excitement. It was not intended for Father's ears but to sit Charley right that he might compare with Mr O's statement. Since then Father stated in one of his letters that he saw an extract from the Evening News[2] on the subject & wanted to know why I did not write. I gave an outline in reply & noted the departure of persons. Mr O. not reaching there mailed the letter & unfortunately it was recd. just at the nick of time.[3] Father was arranging to leave & 4 days after he mailed a letter, requesting a Draft to be sent. It was due there today. I sent a Draft for Mrs Miller[4] which was due there on 19th & wrote at the same time that we were expecting Fathers &c. & in his letter to which the Draft was a reply (due 24th) I've answered to his enquiries as to his return. I wrote that I apprehended no difficulty.[5] The rumors were general & he knows what rumors were afloat about McKinlay[6] & Howard[7] & how it resulted & in the present case it was entitled to the benefit of the same Doubts. I hope this will (with your cogent reasoning) quiet his fears & have him forthcoming. I need a furlough & as soon as I hear will bring his trunk up.

J M F. D.[8] is here. He has impudence enough to take him through. I will reserve further news until I see you.

Mrs Bonneau is at Mrs Westons. We had a murder case last night. A Black stabbed another & cut the throat of an Irish that interfered.[9] It is said that Black is dead [*illegible word*].

The Family joins me in Love. Do look out for a white flag Friday afternoon & Saturday morning & if you see it send the cart down.[10] Father may determine to leave & write to that effect in his reply to letter due there 19th. If not I wont hear until next week.

I am sorry to hear of your extra labor to save the corn for harvest. Wms[11] health may be more impared by it. Hoping you are rid of your headache. I conclude with my Love to the Family, Yourself intended. Yours sincerely

J M Johnson

Should you have any orders
forward without delay, if I hear
I wont stay. J M J

1. Probably Samuel Oakes, the free colored bootmaker. See letter of May 21, 1860, note 7, above.

2. Unfortunately, the Charleston *Evening News* for August and September 1860 has not survived.

3. That is, the letter arrived just as James D. Johnson was preparing to leave for Charleston.

4. Perhaps Gabriella's mother. See letter of September 16, 1860, note 9, above.

5. In other words, James M. Johnson advised his father that he would be allowed to return to Charleston.

6. William McKinlay, the wealthy free colored tailor. See letter of May 14, 1860, note 4, above.

7. Robert Howard was one of the wealthiest free men of color in Charleston. A wood dealer like the Dereefs, he paid city taxes on five slaves and real estate worth $33,900. Apparently both McKinlay and Howard had been allowed to return to Charleston sometime in the past, when it had been rumored that their return would not be permitted. 1860 Population Schedules, Charleston, Ward 3, dwelling 501, SCDAH; *List of the Taxpayers of Charleston, 1860*, 324.

8. John M. F. Dereef was one of the sons of R. E. Dereef. J. M. F. Dereef, like his father, was a wood factor. He was listed in his father's household in the 1860 federal census. He was about thirty years old and paid municipal taxes on real estate worth $3,700. 1860 Population Schedules, Charleston, Ward 5, dwelling 592, SCDAH; *List of the Taxpayers of Charleston, 1860*, 319.

9. According to an account in the *Mercury*, September 24, 1860, Samuel O'Conner attempted to separate some slaves who were fighting on Calhoun Street, near Middle, about 8:30 P.M. O'Conner's neck was slashed by Abraham, one of the slaves; Joe, another slave, was severely cut in the back. O'Conner died almost immediately; Joe's fate was not mentioned.

10. A white flag at the train depot at Claremont would evidently signal that James M. Johnson had arrived.

11. William Ellison, Jr.

Charleston Octr. 8th 1860

Dear Henry

Yours is recd. I am glad to hear that you are well & that there is no serious sickness in the Family. I could not get off as I wished. I am obliged for the trouble you have been at in sending & propose sending Father's Trunk up on Wednesday & following it on Saturday next 13th inst. I had it packed & ready to send off on Thursday but could not get a conveyance for it to RR the rain was so hard. By sending it Wednesday E. Ann may get possession of what she stands in need of sooner than if left until I go.

The Yellow Fever has been here since the last of August. I am truly glad E. Ann did not get to hear of it sooner. It has not been as fatal as in some past years. There has been a number of cases in King St.[1] Koppell,[2] Tailor, has just got better of it & 2 others in the immediate neighborhood. Osborne,[3] Artist, buries his wife to day & the Election[4] & bad spirits will swell the victims. The very dry weather up to Thursday has checked its progress. Poor Mayranz[5] was sick but 2 days. He died on the 3d. I was so shocked when I saw acct of his Death. I went to the House & saw his corpse & then found out it was yellow fever. I had seen him a few days before & was making up to speak to him when he turned a corner.

Mrs Dereef[6] & Miss D.[7] the unengaged passed here to day. Aspinall[8] was quite captivated. I have just heard from Father. He leaves to day for N.Y.[9] We are all well. The Family joins me in Love to you & all at Wisdom Hall. Thine Ever

J M J

1. That is, where Johnson worked in his father's tailor shop.

2. Hermann Koppel was a tailor and sewing machine agent who lived at 306 King Street, just south of Johnson's tailor shop. Koppel, a white man, paid no city property tax in 1860. Ferslew, *Directory of Charleston, 1860*, 88; Ford, *Census of Charleston, 1861*, 121.

3. J. M. Osborn was a photographer whose office was at 223 King Street. Osborn was a white man; he paid no city property taxes in 1860. Ferslew, *Directory of Charleston, 1860*, 38.

4. The biennial election of state legislators was scheduled for October 8 and 9. Johnson speculated that bad liquor, which was freely distributed on election days, would increase the number of yellow fever victims. Charleston *Mercury*, October 8, 1860.

5. Probably John Mayrant, a

free colored carpenter about thirty-eight years old who was propertyless. 1850 Population Schedules, Charleston, Ward 4, dwelling 191, SCDAH.

6. Mary Dereef, the wife of Joseph Dereef.

7. One of Joseph Dereef's daughters; see letter of August 20, 1860, notes 40, 42, 44, above.

8. Probably the free colored tailor, Albert Aspinall. See the letter of August 20, 1860, note 26, above.

9. James D. Johnson was leaving Canada for New York, on his way back to Charleston.

Charleston Octr 12/60

Dear Henry

Yours of 11th is recd & contents noted. I got Mr Desverney[1] to attend to shipping the Trunk after pointing it out to Mr Pinckney.[2] [*That*] is the cause of its not being prepaid & I was in a hurry to get to the shop. I regret that you had the trouble of sending twice.[3]

Mr Hoff[4] being sick I am disappointed again. I have not heard from Father since last Saturday. I will make another attempt to get off on Tuesday. I suppose Mr Hoff will be out by then.

Business is getting brisk. We find it impracticable to collect any dues to carry it on & have to resort to credit. The travellers are returning.[5] A great many, to avoid the risk of fever, spend their evenings at Summerville[6] & return in the morning to the city. The health of the city is not bad, the mortality being small compared to the sick list.

I see Moody more than doubled Wacter.[7] The fighting managers are getting betters. Wharton[8] who was worst off is the man who built the Tidal Drains.[9] White[10] is stone cutter's brother, both bullys.

I will bring up those articles you wrote for. The Family joins me in Love. No more at present yrs truly

J M Johnson

1. Probably Peter Desverney, the free man of color who obtained his freedom by informing his master, John Prioleau, of the Denmark Vesey plot in 1822. In addition to his freedom, Desverney received an annual pension from the state larger than that granted to any other South Carolinian. In 1860 Desverney lived on St. Philip Street, not far from the railroad depot. Kennedy and Parker, *Report of the Insurrection,* 48–49; Means and Turnbull, *Charleston Directory, 1859,* 54.

2. Probably John Pinckney, a free man of color about forty years old who was a porter.

Charleston Free Negro Tax Book, 1862, CLS.

3. Henry had to send somebody to the Claremont depot twice. On the first trip to pick up the trunk, the person—probably one of Ellison's slaves—discovered the trunk was not prepaid and had to return to the Ellisons' to get the amount due for the freight charge, then go back and get the trunk.

4. John Hoff was a forty-four-year-old free mulatto tailor who, it appears from this statement, worked in Johnson's tailor shop. See letter of January 20, 1860, note 17, above.

5. Charlestonians who could afford it left the city during the summer months to escape the oppressive heat and the dangers of disease. Many of those who were returning, Johnson pointed out, still did not risk staying overnight in the city.

6. See letter of August 20, 1860, note 39, above.

7. Although it has proved impossible to identify Wacter, the Moody referred to was probably a member of the large Moody family living near the Ellisons in Stateburg. See letter of May 5, 1860, note 11, above.

8. George C. Wharton was a white man, a brickmason, who lived on America Street. He paid no city property taxes in 1860. Ferslew, *Directory of Charleston, 1860*, 130.

9. The tidal drains were a sewer system designed to drain the marshy land in the city to reduce the risk of disease. A new set of drains was constructed during the administration of Mayor William Porcher Miles and was an issue in Charles Macbeth's first election as mayor in 1857. See, for example, William Porcher Miles's "Report on City Affairs," Charleston *Mercury*, October 14, 1857.

10. Robert D. White owned a marble and stone yard at 123 Meeting Street. Edwin R. White worked there. Both were white. Johnson was apparently referring to one of these men or to a brother of one of them. Edwin White paid city taxes on one slave and one dog; Robert D. White paid no city taxes in 1860. Ferslew, *Directory of Charleston, 1860*, 141; *List of the Taxpayers of Charleston, 1860*, 299.

Charleston So Ca Oct 31st
[*1860*]

Dear Henry

This will inform you that I got my children[1] off this morning by the Marrion.[2] They left this morning at 7 o'clock. They are comfortable provide for, having a state room and I believe a kind capt which have promise to put them aboard of the cars for Philadelphia under the care of the conductor. The stewardess has promise to take good care of them. I gave her a trifle so as to incourage her. I hope God will be with them and protect them. I am quite worried down.

I tried every plan and made every effort to get them off on board of the Keystone State[3] but the agents took a stand and would not deviate although Messrs Adams & Frost[4] interested themselves much to effect a passage. They positively wont take any free colored person unless there are cleared out of the coustom house by some white person as there slaves.[5] Then of course they cannot get a state room. The captain of the Key Stone State[6] verry kindly offered to take care of them if I should send them as above but I would not agree to send them as slaves when they are not and besides they might not be taken care of.[7]

I wrote by Monday's night mail to Miss Forten[8] and to Monsier Barguet[9] in New York informing them that I would send them by the Marrion. If they get the letter they will be on the look out for them. Inform Father and Sister[10] that they are gone.

Tell Father that the cotton have arrived and sampled but was not sold.[11] This morning I was at the office quite early this morning. They had no offers when I was there.

The Friends are generally well. Miss Rosamon Lee[12] have been in bed for some months with consumation. Mrs Weston[13] Also have been confine to bed, her daughter tells me for three months. I took the children to see them Monday after noon but did not see her. Mr Johnson[14] is well. Mrs Johnson[15] is not at home.

I hope you and all are well. I expect to leave Saturday. You will send for me that day. Your affectionate brother

Wm Ellison Jr.

1. William Ellison, Jr., had three living children in 1860: William John, who was fourteen years old; Elizabeth Anna, who was twelve or thirteen; and Henrietta Inglis, who was ten or eleven. Whether all of the children were put aboard the *Marion* cannot be determined. 1860 Population Schedules, Sumter, dwellings 694, 695, 696, SCDAH; Ellison family

graveyard, Stateburg.

2. The steamer *Marion* was scheduled to leave Adger's wharves for New York at precisely the time William said. The captain of the *Marion* was S. Whiting. Charleston *Mercury*, October 30, 1860.

3. The *Keystone State* was the steamer to Philadelphia, the ultimate destination of William's children. It sailed from North Atlantic Wharf at 5 P.M. on October 30. The agents were Thomas S. and Thomas G. Budd, white commission merchants whose offices were on North Atlantic Wharf. Thomas S. Budd paid city taxes on three slaves; Thomas G. paid taxes as the trustee of real estate worth $8,000. Ferslew, *Directory of Charleston, 1860*, 45; *List of the Taxpayers of Charleston, 1860*, 38; Charleston *Mercury*, October 30, 1860.

4. The offices of the Ellisons' factors on Adger's North Wharf were separated from the North Atlantic Wharf, from which the *Keystone State* departed, by the Atlantic or Central Wharf. Ford, *Census of Charleston, 1861*, 224–25.

5. The Budds' position was understandable. If they allowed a free colored person to leave who turned out in fact to be a slave, then they, the agents, were guilty of having aided a slave to run away, an offense punishable by death without benefit of clergy. Only months earlier Francis Michel, a young white porter from New York who worked aboard the *Marion*, had been sentenced to be executed for aiding the slave of a Charleston butcher to run away. After months of imprisonment, Michel was pardoned just before his execution date in March 1861. If William had agreed to allow his children to be claimed as the slaves of some white person, then the Budds would not be culpable, as a slaveowner was of course allowed to take his slaves with him wherever he went. The Budds' caution on this matter reflected the tensions in Charleston as the secession crisis deepened—Lincoln's election was to come within the next week. O'Neall, *Negro Law of South Carolina*, 45; Charleston *Courier*, January 30, 1860.

6. The captain's name was Marshman. Charleston *Mercury*, October 30, 1860.

7. William's decision was wise; his worry, legitimate. Nothing save the good will of the white person to whom William might have claimed his children were enslaved would have prevented the person from in fact treating them as slaves, even selling them.

8. Probably Miss Margaretta Forten, who since 1845 had headed the Lombard Street Primary School in Philadelphia, a private school for Negroes.

Like her father James Forten, a prominent Negro abolitionist who died in 1842, Margaretta was active in antislavery causes, serving for many years as secretary of the Philadelphia Female Anti-Slavery Society. It is unlikely that the slaveholding Ellisons and the abolitionist Fortens were old friends, but just how the Ellisons knew of Miss Forten and her school and how William, Jr., was able to make the complicated arrangements so quickly is not clear. We do know, however, that Margaretta's younger sister, Harriet, had married South Carolina-born Robert Purvis, the son of an English immigrant and a "woman of Moroccan descent," almost certainly a "Turk" from the Stateburg area. It is also possible that Mr. Barguet (see note 9, below) made all of the arrangements for William Ellison, Jr. We cannot determine if the Ellison children actually enrolled in the Lombard Street Primary School because the two roll books that are extant cover only the period from 1843 to 1850 (years in which no Ellisons appear). However, Forten's school would have been a logical choice for William Ellison's children, since it was the only one that took free colored children as "boarding scholars," according to a contemporary survey of the free colored community in Philadelphia. For information on the enrollment records of Forten's school, we are indebted to Barbara Simons of the Historical Society of Pennsylvania. Lewis, "The Fortens of Philadelphia"; Billington, ed., *The Journal of Charlotte Forten*; Bacon, *Statistics of the Colored People of Philadelphia*, 8.

9. The Barguet (or Barquet) family had lived in Charleston for many years. In 1807 John P. Barquet was admitted to the Brown Fellowship Society and in 1830 his son of the same name was also admitted. As late as 1855 Edward Barquet was living on St. Michael's Alley, between Church and Meeting Streets. No Barquet was listed in the Free Negro Tax Books after 1855. Ellison was certainly referring to a member of the Barquet family who was in New York, but it is impossible to be certain which member. Although no Barquet appears in the New York City directories between 1856 and 1862, an 1857 letter from the city written by a free man of color formerly of Charleston mentions a Bissett Barguet, who lives in New York but plans to emigrate to Jamaica. List of Members of the Brown Fellowship Society, RSSL; Charleston Free Negro Tax Books, 1816–1862, SCDAH, LC, CLS; Edward Hollo-

way to Charles Holloway,
March 16, 1857, Holloway
Scrapbook, RSSL.

10. Eliza Ann Johnson,
James M. Johnson's wife.

11. According to his report
to the federal census marshal
August 22, 1860, William Ellison, Sr., made eighty bales of
cotton in 1859. When he died
in 1861 his estate included 100
bales of cotton. 1860 Agricultural Schedules, Sumter, 21,
SCDAH; Appraisement and Inventory, December 21, 1861,
William Ellison Estate Papers,
Box 151, Package 8, Sumter
County Estate Papers, SCDAH.

12. Rosamond Lee was the
twenty-one-year-old daughter of

the tailor and prominent free
man of color, John Lee. On
Lee, see letter of August 20,
1860, note 17, above.

13. Probably Louisa P.
Weston. Her daughter Mary
was about seventeen in 1860.
1860 Population Schedules,
Charleston, Ward 5, dwelling
188, SCDAH.

14. James D. Johnson had
safely returned to Charleston.
James M. Johnson was probably in Stateburg. His letter of
October 12, 1860, above, indicated his intention to go to
Stateburg as soon as John Hoff
returned to work.

15. Delia Johnson, the wife
of James D. Johnson.

Charleston Decr 7th/60

Dear Henry

I was about to write & enquire as to the mode of forwarding your pants & vests when on my way from the Artesian well[1] when I accosted a Drayman who told me of an engagement he had for the morning to take Cain[2] to the Depot[3] so that I concluded to avail myself of that opportunity to send the pants & vest. I have selected some thing warm & I think it will prove serviceable.

The excitement has not abated.[4] The tone of the President's message will give force to their resolve.[5] There being no fear of an attempt at coercion they will lose sight of more remote consequences.

In the Legislature they have not lost sight of us. The chrmn of our Committee J. H. R. Esqr,[6] in view of the opposition & by way of killing Mr Eason's Bill[7] (which by the way is [located] at Anthony Westons),[8] sent down for the Tax Book[9] with a request to have it sent by a respectable cold. man. Robt. Houston[10] was selected by the Gentleman. The Despatch was sent to [*him*], but as it was Saturday night he could not leave his charge (Grace Church). He got Jn De Large[11] to take it up by Night Train & as a counter move Mr Eason came down & got a Petition signed by 800,[12] with which he has returned & put a clause to the Bill prohibiting them from carrying on Business through an Agent or Guardian with which addition he made a favorable report.[13] De Large returned on Tuesday. There was no business done Monday on acct of the College Graduates.[14] Wednesday an effort was made by Jn Lee[15] & Jacob Weston[16] to get a counter petition signed. They succeeded with the Aristocrats & it is presented by Mr De Saussure[17] as the Petition of Prest. Jas Rose[18] & others in behalf of free persons of color &c. Mr. Morrison[19] from our committee has also reported favorably on a Bill to prevent slaves & free persons of color from riding in coaches &c. I hope the use of the City Railway[20] will be granted to passengers from Depot, it being so far. The fate of the above bills is undecided. Mr Weston told me that the [*number of*] signatures would not compare with the one in favor of the Bill, but it was signed by the most respectable citisens so that what it lacked in numbers was made up in respectability. The Bill to leave in 1862 being lost, this is to accomplish the same result.[21]

The Election for Delegates[22] came off yesterday. The vote polled was nearly as large as that for Representatives.[23] I saw a melee at one of the polls between a customer of ours & others. I did not wait to see the result.

Rev Mr. Prentiss[24] preached a sermon at St Peters which he repeated at Columbia & was then called to deliver at the Hall of the House of Representatives on Tuesday night.[25] One of its distinguishing features is the inferiority of the Race.

The Synod[26] met here last week. I heard Messrs McQueen[27] & McDowell[28] of Sumter. Dr. Witherspoon[29] was in attendance. I saw Bishop Davis.[30] He preached at St. Luke's on Sunday.

Father & Mag[31] tenders their respects. I will send a few papers. Yrs truly

J M Johnson

Mr. H. Ellison
Stateburg, S.C.

1. The well was on Wentworth Street, near Meeting.

2. Dr. D. J. Cain lived on Wentworth, near the intersection with Meeting. A white man, he paid city taxes on six slaves and income of $7,000. Ferslew, *Directory of Charleston, 1860*, 48; *List of the Taxpayers of Charleston, 1860*, 43; Ford, *Census of Charleston, 1861*, 219; 1860 Population Schedules, Charleston, Ward 3, dwelling 230, SCDAH.

3. The railroad depot in Charleston.

4. The campaign for the secession of South Carolina was in full force.

5. In his annual message of December 3, President James Buchanan blamed the North for agitation of the slavery question, conceded the legitimacy of southern grievances, and proposed a constitutional convention to remedy the situation. Although he argued that he lacked the authority to "coerce" a state, he warned that secession amounted to revolution and was illegal, and he reaffirmed his duty to uphold the law. As David M. Potter has written, his speech was "a curious combination of realism and fantasy." Secessionists tended to interpret it as Johnson suggested in the letter. Potter, *The Impending Crisis*, 519–21.

6. John Harleston Read, Jr., chairman of the Committee on the Colored Population in the General Assembly, represented the low country district of Prince George Winyaw. For his defense of free persons of color, see note 9, below.

7. James M. Eason led the campaign of the white working-men of Charleston to eliminate free persons of color as competitors in the job market. Eason was a machinist who operated a large foundry not far from Joseph Dereef's house. In 1860 Eason paid city taxes on six slaves of his own and real estate worth $14,500; he also paid taxes on another twelve slaves

and $12,000 worth of real estate owned by the foundry he held jointly with his brother, Thomas D. Eason. During the campaign for the legislature in late September and early October, Eason and Henry T. Peake presented themselves as representatives of the interests of the white workingmen. Like Eason, Peake was a successful white mechanic. He was the superintendent of the large workshop of the South Carolina Railroad near Joseph Dereef's house. Peake paid city taxes on nine slaves and real estate worth $4,500, but he must have had considerable holdings outside the city, as he reported real estate worth $10,000 and personal property worth $52,600 to the federal census.

Eason and Peake attacked both free persons of color and their white protectors. They promised to support the interests of white workingmen "whenever questions arise in which their rights and interests come in conflict with *free* negroes—negroes, free in *fact*, but held by *trustees*, and slaves hiring their own time—plague spots in this community, affecting pecuniarily and socially, only working men. . . . The learned professions being closed against the negro, as also all mercantile pursuits, they have been thrust on the working men only as competitors (a system

which has driven nearly all our young mechanics from their homes)." Eason and Peake supporters argued that representatives who were not workingmen would promise to protect their interests, "but 'twill be such protection (when it conflicts with the rights of this privileged class of negroes) as vultures give to lambs." Smoldering racial and class animosities lay behind this appeal. As a supporter of Eason and Peake pointed out, "Professional men who have never done a day's work, may talk of the *dignity of labor*, and deem their listeners fools; but has any *white mechanic* ever felt this dignity of labor when unsuccessful in estimating for a job, he finds that it has been awarded to one of our *very respectable free persons of color*, from whom, also, an estimate has been obtained; thus, adding to his disappointment, the mortification of feeling that this *dignity of labor places him alone* on the same level with this highly valued and privileged class of negroes." Eason and Peake were easily elected, with overwhelming majorities in the white working-class area of the city north of Calhoun. Eason polled the third highest number of votes among the thirty-six candidates. He managed to get appointed to the Committee on the Colored Population and presented a bill to prohibit all free persons of color from carrying on any mechanical pursuit on their own account and from entering into any contract for mechanical work. In effect, this bill would have prohibited free persons of color from working as anything other than hired hands or domestic servants. Eason also orchestrated support for his bill among the white workingmen of Charleston. For example, just after the legislature convened, the following advertisement appeared in the *Mercury*:

MR. EASON'S FREE NEGRO BILL—TO MECHANICS, WORKING MEN AND ALL WHITE MEN WHO LIVE BY THE SWEAT OF THEIR BROW —Your attention is called to the notice of a bill, introduced into the Legislature by your Representative, Jas. M. Eason, Esq., for the protection of the rights and interests of your class. From none could such a bill be more properly presented and defended—himself a practical working man, who, in his daily avocation, has repeatedly been made to feel the hardship and injustice of having the entire free negro population thrust upon us and our children as competitors—all other avocations being protected by legal en-

actments. This bill will, as you may suppose, meet with strong opposition from some of those gentlemen, who by their calling or profession, are neither subjected to the degradation of such competition, or can feel that the working man has any right to similar protection with themselves against it. For the first time one of our own Representatives has dared to meet the issue. It is for you to say whether you will, by your earnest support and action, sustain him, or by your supineness and indifference show to those who disregard our demand for justice in this matter, that we know our rights but dare not maintain them. Let us be doing. The entering wedge is made; let us, by wholesome and well-directed blows, split from our body politic this cankerous sore, and stand among our fellow-citizens as equals. We ask nothing more.

MECHANIC

Charleston *Mercury*, September 25, 29, October 11, November 30, 1860; 1860 Population Schedules, Charleston, Ward 7, dwelling 344; Ward 8, dwelling 542, SCDAH; *List of the Taxpayers of Charleston, 1860*, 84, 218.

8. It was probably not a coincidence that a copy of Eason's

bill was available at Anthony Weston's house on Calhoun Street for the perusal of the free colored community. Weston, after all, was a "very respectable free colored person" who was a millwright. On Weston, see letter of September 3, 1860, note 2, above.

9. The city tax book listed the municipal taxes paid by all the residents of Charleston. The strategy of Read and the opponents of Eason's bill was evidently to demonstrate the property ownership and respectability of the free persons of color in Charleston in contrast to that of their enemies among the white workingmen in the city. Indeed, when Read reported his opposition to the bill to sell all free persons of color in the state after January 1, 1862, he specifically noted that the free persons of color in the state were "good citizens, and patterns of industry, sobriety and irreproachable conduct," according to the Columbia correspondent of the Baltimore *Sun*. Although Read's report has not survived, the *Sun*'s account suggests the use Read made of the Charleston tax book taken to Columbia by John De Large: "He says that there is at present within the borders of the State nearly ten thousand free colored persons; that they are thrifty, orderly, and well disposed; that they are the owners of a vast amount of property, both real

and personal; that in the City of Charleston alone they pay taxes on $1,561,870 worth of property; that of this amount *more than three hundred thousand dollars are in slaves*; that the free negroes of Charleston alone pay taxes to the amount of $27,209.18, and that other portions of the state show as fair a ratio." [Italics in the original.] According to the *Sun* correspondent, the report's concluding sentences were a ringing defense of free persons of color in the name of justice and humanity: "Whilst we are battling for our rights, liberties, and institutions, can we expect the smiles and counternance [*sic*] of the Arbiter of all events when we make war upon the impotent and unprotected, enslave them against all justice? God forbid that this Legislature could tolerate such a sentiment—forbid it, humanity—condemn it, enlightened legislation."

The bill Read spoke against declared all free persons of color within the state after January 1, 1862, "to be slaves to all intents and purposes." Such persons were to be taken into custody by the sheriffs of the various districts in the state and sold to the highest bidder. The law allowed any free person of color to choose a master for himself and become a slave of that person until the January 1 deadline. The editor of the *Mercury* opposed this bill as "harsh in its policy, and wholly unrequired by the public exigencies, while it is mischievous in its effects, and remarkably ill-timed in its promulgation." Another opponent wrote the *Mercury* that he regarded free persons of color "as a safe class of people, who will keep their eyes and ears open to give us warning of any danger, and we should be both sorry and ashamed to see any act of the Legislature passed to reduce them to slavery, or to drive them with ruinous haste from our borders." Needless to say, white workingmen in Charleston did not express their opposition to this bill. Baltimore *Sun*, December 18, 1860; Charleston *Mercury*, November 24 and 27, 1860.

10. A year earlier Houston had thanked C. G. Memminger for his defense of free persons of color in the legislature. See letter of January 9, 1860, note 12, above.

11. De Large, a free colored tailor and steward, also worshipped at Grace Church. See letter of August 28, 1860, note 31, above.

12. The petition passionately embellished the themes Eason had emphasized in his legislative campaign. It read, in part:

Petition of the Mechanics, Artisans, and others of the city of Charleston, praying the enactment of a law to prevent free negroes or persons of color from carrying on any trade, calling, or occupation, in their own name or the name of others. . . .

That it is a prevailing and common practice, in the City of Charleston, for free negroes and persons of color to carry on and conduct mechanical and other pursuits as contractors and masters.

That it is also common for slaves to do the same thing, sometimes, and not infrequently, in their own names, and sometimes in the names and under the nominal, and merely nominal, cover and protection of white persons or free persons of color.

Your petitioners show to your Honorable Body that these are serious public evils and a great grievance to your petitioners especially. . . .

Under the existing state of law, every other pursuit, except such as your petitioners are engaged in, where skill and intelligence are required, above what is necessary to the mere laborer, is carefully protected by stringent enactments of law against the intrusion of the colored and slave races.

The merchant is not allowed to employ his slave, or a free negro or colored person, as his clerk; so, too, is it of the wharfinger, of the lawyer, of the doctor, of the tradesman, and the store-keeper, all these avocations, and all others, whatever they may be, are, as your petitioners understand it, protected by law from the intrusion of the colored race. The law does not show them the chance of an equality, and it makes a penal offense for those who attempt it in any other pursuit, except in the mechanic arts. This is unjust and unfair. It might be enough to say that all laws which are unjust and unfair, are public evils.

But your petitioners further show, as a fact, that under the operation of these laws, the colored races, excluded from other pursuits, have been tempted—in fact, driven—to become mechanics, and have taken the place, in a large extent, of the intelligent white youths, who, in former times, selected such pursuits as avocations for life, by which they would hope to rise in position, respectability, and independence among their fellow citizens. The reason of this effect of the operation of the law is manifest. It is because they are placed upon a footing of unequal rivalry with the colored race; and this the white race among us does not, and ought not to be expected to consent to.

Is not that a public evil which compels the citizen, or any one of the dominant race, to abandon the pursuit of his choice, or to place himself in competition and rivalry upon an apparently equal footing with the servile or colored race?—a rivalry too, where the chances of success are unequal, unless he will reduce his manner of living, his deportment, and personal bearing to the level of a menial.

Is there any one so hardy as to say that it is good policy to reduce any portion of our white population, or to elevate any portion of our colored population to equal condition and standing. . . .

And this, your petitioners say, is not only a public evil, but is to them a great and sore grievance, imposed upon them by the operation of laws which afford protection to other pursuits, and unjustly and unfairly denies it to theirs.

The negro or colored person, whether free or slave, who has the capacity to succeed as a master mechanic, even in the humblest of the mechanic arts, and to conduct such business, has also the capacity to succeed as a merchant, a merchant's clerk, as a tradesman, or a shopkeeper, and even in what are called the learned professions. Why then should he not be permitted to exercise his capacity in those different callings, if he is allowed to enter in a fair and equal competition with the mechanic? The reason is obvious.

There should be no distinction unless the law and lawgiver intend to declare that the mechanic is not the equal of the merchant, the lawyer, the doctor, the wharfinger, the tradesman, or the shopkeeper.

Why then are the laws so shaped as to exemplify this idea of superiority and inferiority? Is it wise to tax the loyalty of the working poor man, by such discriminations to the institution which he is educated to defend, and in the defense of which he is always the foremost?

Charleston *Mercury*, December 12, 1860.

13. The amendment to prohibit free persons of color from doing business "either by himself, agent, or guardian" closed a loophole through which free persons of color with strong white allies might have been able to escape the operation of the proposed law. With the amendment, the prohibition on the kinds of work done by nearly all the men among the free colored elite was virtually ironclad. Eason introduced his amendment on Wednesday, De-

cember 5. Charleston *Mercury*, December 6, 1860.

14. Graduation exercises of the South Carolina College in Columbia were held Monday, December 3.

15. The prominent free colored steward; see the letter of August 20, note 17, above.

16. The well-known free colored tailor; see the letter of June 25, 1855, note 2, above.

17. Wilmot Gibbes DeSaussure was a member of the Charleston delegation in the General Assembly. DeSaussure was an attorney who lived at 31 East Bay. In 1860 he paid municipal taxes on four slaves and real estate worth $5,000. It has proved impossible to locate the petition DeSaussure presented. Ferslew, *Directory of Charleston, 1860*, 60; *List of the Taxpayers of Charleston, 1860*, 74.

18. James Rose, who lived at 74 Broad, was the president of the South West Rail Road Bank. Rose reported to the federal census real estate worth $10,000 and personal property worth $1,200. He paid municipal taxes on fifteen slaves. Ferslew, *Directory of Charleston, 1860*, 120; *List of the Taxpayers of Charleston*, 245; 1860 Population Schedules, Charleston, Ward 2, dwelling 366, SCDAH.

19. Richard Tillard Morrison represented the low country district of St. James Santee in the General Assembly. His bill was

reported out of the Committee
on the Colored Population with
Eason's bill on December 6.
The presentments of the
Charleston Grand Jury at its
January term in 1860 included

> as a nuisance, which calls
> loudly for a remedy, the rid-
> ing in public carriages and
> other vehicles of free negroes
> and slaves, and in many cases
> driven by white men; it is
> proper that the line of demar-
> cation between the castes
> should be clear and distinct,
> more particularly at this time,
> for reasons which need not be
> mentioned here. It is fully
> time that slaves and free per-
> sons of color should know
> and understand their posi-
> tion, and we hope that a most
> stringent law will be passed
> subjecting the owners of such
> vehicles to a fine, and the oc-
> cupants of the seats, whether
> bond or free, be subject
> to corporeal punishment.

Charleston *Courier*, January 13,
1860; Charleston *Mercury*, December 7, 1860.

20. The transit system within
the city of Charleston.

21. Johnson's point was that
if the bill requiring that all free
persons of color in the state in
January 1862 be sold into slavery failed to pass, Eason's bill
would accomplish the same end,
namely getting rid of all free
persons of color.

22. The election of delegates
to the convention that would
decide whether South Carolina
would secede was held December 6, 1860. The election had
been called by a special session
of the state legislature that
agreed to the bill for the election on November 10, three
days after Lincoln's election.

23. Indeed, the turnout for
the election was about 25 percent greater than that for the
October election to the legislature, which itself was a near record turnout. It lacked only forty
votes of reaching the level of the
1856 legislative vote, the highest ever recorded in the city.
Charleston *Courier*, October 16,
1860; Charleston *Mercury*, December 8, 1860.

24. Reverend William O.
Prentiss was an Episcopal
clergyman who was ordained in
1846, after spending time as
an assistant at St. Peter's in
Charleston, "giving much attention to the work among the
Negroes," according to Thomas,
A Historical Account, 249.
Prentiss also served a parish on
the South Edisto River and,
from 1866 to 1868, Calvary
Church in Charleston, a nearly
all-Negro congregation. Ibid.,
167, 202, 227, 438, 646.

25. Prentiss delivered the sermon in St. Peter's on November
21, again on November 25, and
a third time before the legislature on December 4. The ser-

mon rehearsed the historical and Biblical arguments for slavery, lambasted abolitionist fanatics, and called passionately for secession. As Johnson noted, Prentiss also spelled out his views on the capacities of Negroes:

We must digress for awhile, to ascertain what history, physiology, and experience teach us of the capacity of the African race for freedom and self-government. History assures us that this race has been, from its earliest records, a nation of slaves, and that the African has joyfully acquiesced in slavery as his normal condition. Physiology proves that he is utterly ungovernable by men of his own race. Experience teaches us, that he is totally uninfluenced by even white teachers of morality, politics, arts, or anything else, unless the instructor becomes a personal acquaintance, and the degree of the teacher's influence is exactly proportioned to the length and intimacy of such acquaintance. . . . If time allowed me to develop these truths, I could prove to you that this constitution, divinely implanted in the African, renders him an efficient, a contented, a willing laborer under the direction of the white man; and I could demonstrate the absurdity of believing that dangerous combinations could be formed by him with badly disposed white persons, with whom our police regulations do not permit him to be intimately acquainted. . . . These are facts, with which our enemies [are] unacquainted (yet theorizing in ignorance and defiance thereof) [and] propose to overthrow; and, acknowledging the obligation of moral suasion only, they undertake to launch the African into a state of existence which shall ruin him as a reliable cultivator of tropical products, totally incapacitate him for religion, entail unhappiness and degradation upon himself, and ultimate confusion and anarchy upon the communities of his residence, which shall overthrow, if successful, God's purpose and decree in his behalf, that a servant of servants he shall be to his brethren.

Prentiss, *A Sermon*, 12–13.

26. The Presbyterian Synod of South Carolina convened in Charleston on November 29, 1860. Charleston *Mercury*, November 30, 1860.

27. Reverend D. McQueen, one of the delegates to the synod, was a member of the Committee on Bills and Overtures and presented a series of measures

for the synod's consideration on November 30, 1860. Charleston *Mercury*, December 1, 1860.

28. Reverend J. McDowell was a delegate to the synod. Charleston *Mercury*, November 30, 1860.

29. Dr. J. B. Witherspoon was a wealthy sixty-year-old white physician from Sumter District. 1860 Population Schedules, Sumter, dwelling 980, SCDAH.

30. Bishop of the Diocese of South Carolina; see the letter of January 9, 1860, note 2, above.

31. Margaret, James M. Johnson's cousin.

Charleston Decr 19/60

My Dear Friend

I have recd your favor of the 10th. It had to be dried before it could be read, being wet from the decay of the potatoes. I am quite obliged to you & William for the Potatoes & regret very much that they did not reach me in the order you sent them. They were too fine to have been kept at the Depot to rot. The neglect must have been on the Agt[1] part as I had Gabriel[2] to enquire repeatedly. I sent Grant[3] with the receipt & it was delivered. By cutting off the rot we were able to get some good fragments & shared them with Mrs Bonneau. She sent her thanks & invited me to call & see the Baby. I judge Mrs H.[4] must have a little one.

As it regards Emigration your humble Servt is on the alert with the whole of our people who are debating where to go. The majority are in favor of Hayti.[5] Some few are leaving here by each Steamer.[6] Dont suppose I will be the last because I have replaced a missing tree.[7] I only want to beautify the exterior so as to attract Capitalists.

The Convention[8] is in full blast & Legislature[9] meets tomorrow. The Mechanics Bill[10] is thought to be gone to Old Nick & now my Dear Friend with our regards to your Father & Brothers I am yr sincere Friend

J D Johnson

Dear Henry

I recd yours & regret that we all have such cause for uneasiness. I enclose an extract you may not have seen. Please send for me to the Depot on Monday next. I may possibly come up on the 9 o'clock train. Thine ever

J M Johnson

1. The agent at the railroad or express depot apparently misplaced the potatoes.

2. Probably a slave belonging to James D. Johnson. In 1860 he paid municipal taxes on three slaves. *List of the Taxpayers of Charleston, 1860,* 324.

3. Probably another slave belonging to Johnson. See letter of April 24, 1860, note 5, above.

4. Mrs. Bonneau's daughter, Frances P. (Bonneau) Holloway, who was living with her. See letters of February 14, 1852, note 6 and January 20, 1860, note 3, above.

5. The government of Haiti actively encouraged the emigration of American Negroes. Immigrants were promised a homestead, tools for working the land, and food and shelter from the time they arrived on

the island until they had managed to get settled. But above
all Haiti promised a homeland
for Afro-Americans. As the
General Agent of Emigration to
Haiti, James Redpath—the
American abolitionist—wrote
in his *Guide to Hayti*, "Pride of
race, self-respect, social ambi-
tion, parental love, the madness
of the South, the meanness of
the North, the inhumanity of
the Union, and the inclemency
of Canada—all say to the Black
and the man of color, Seek elsewhere a home and a nation-
ality." Hundreds of refugees
from both the North and South
went to Haiti, including some
from Charleston. But once there
they had a hard time getting the
government to deliver on any of
its promises. Redpath, ed., *A
Guide to Hayti*, 172; James Redpath Papers, Manuscript Division, LC; *Douglass' Monthly*,
January 1861, 386–87; April
1861, 437.

6. Between the August en-
slavement crisis and the firing
on Fort Sumter the following
April, hundreds of free people
of color left Charleston. The
correspondent of the New York
Tribune in Philadelphia reported early in November that
780 free persons of color had left
since August and 200 had recently arrived in Philadelphia,
"where their light complexions
and sober behavior have attracted much attention." The

report filed by the Philadelphia
correspondent was a substan-
tially accurate account of recent
events in Charleston and portrayed the sentiments of this
group of refugees:

In 1822, South Carolina
forbade negro emancipation.
In August last, more hostile
laws were enacted against the
free colored race, stimulated
by John Brown's inroad, and
the subsequent symptoms of
an ultimate Republican President. Each free negro was required to have a guardian, to
whom he was assessed as a
slave. He must also wear a
copper badge bearing his
number. If found without a
guardian, he was sold pub-
licly as a slave; if he neglected
to procure the degrading
badge, he was fined $20, and
if caught without it he was
fined and imprisoned. If the
guardian proved to be a dis-
honest man, he would sell
him into perpetual slavery,
after which, his property was
liable to seizure. The law not
only regarded him as a slave,
but actually made him so. Its
object must have been to reduce him to slavery, or to
drive him out of the State.
The latter result has been ac-
complished, for hundreds of
free blacks have been leaving
for the North, and it is probable that all who can raise the

means to come this way, will follow their example. . . . Among those [who have arrived in Philadelphia] are carpenters, masons, shoemakers, tailors, &c., and among the females are milliners, mantuamakers, nurses, &c. Many bring certificates of character and qualification. All have been driven suddenly out of employments by which they gained a living, and are now seeking, under great disadvantages, to begin life anew. Many had acquired real estate and other property, but in the haste to get away were compelled to sell at great loss, while of what they leave behind unsold, they fully expect to be cheated. Some leave relations behind them—an old mother, a decrepid [*sic*] father—whom they are unable to bring away. Some have brought with them their copper badges, which read thus: Charleston, 1860, Servant, 1243. This compulsory exodus reminds us of the revocation of the Edict of Nantz [*sic*], or the expulsion of the Jews from their Ethiopian homes.

The garbled account of the laws in this report probably reflected the confusion of the refugees about the precise legal basis of the enslavement crisis in Charleston. This confusion was seized upon by the *Southern Presbyterian* which responded, in an account reprinted in the *Courier*:

It is not true that there is any law in South Carolina, or in Charleston, requiring the free people of color to wear a distinctive badge, and therefore it is not true that they are emigrating to Philadelphia for that reason. In 1820 South Carolina forbade the emancipation of any slave unless he or she were at the same time removed from the State. Many a slave, however, has, under the easy yoke they wear, been able to accumulate money enough to buy himself free, and many a kind-hearted owner has sought to set free his faithful slave. Accordingly there has grown up a system of nominal ownership, under which the slave has enjoyed the privileges of a free man. Numbers of these persons have recently been returning themselves to the city tax collector as free people, and, the matter attracting the notice of authorities, was inquired into, and of course produced considerable alarm amongst that class. Their emancipation was illegal, and was but nominal. Their only safety was the honor of their nominal owner, and his creditors might make that of no avail.

They chose accordingly to emigrate elsewhere. This is the true account of the matter. There is no general law which will not bear hardly upon individuals and particular classes. The good of the whole community, both white and black, at the South, requires that the two races sustain their present relations to one another. And hence South Carolina forbids emancipation on the soil.

Although this summary of the law was essentially accurate, it was hardly a "true account" of the character of the refugees, many of whom were not in violation of the 1820 law, as this letter and the next one make clear. A careful comparison of the 1860 federal census schedules and the 1860 Free Negro Tax Book with the 1861 city census and the 1862 Free Negro Tax Book confirms that the refugees from Charleston numbered over a thousand. New York *Tribune*, November 10, 1860; Charleston *Courier*, November 19, 1860; Philadelphia *Evening Bulletin*, November 2, 1860.

7. Johnson's houses at 7 and 9 Coming had not been sold; they had been up for sale since before he left for Canada. See letter of September 3, 1860, note 39, above.

8. Indeed, the next afternoon at 1:15 the convention delegates unanimously adopted the resolution "To dissolve the Union between the State of South Carolina and other States united with her under the compact entitled 'The Constitution of the United States of America'." Charleston *Mercury*, December 21, 1860.

9. An outbreak of smallpox in Columbia and secessionist fervor in Charleston caused the legislature to adjourn in Columbia and reconvene in Charleston.

10. Johnson's intelligence about Eason's bill was correct; neither it nor any of the other proscriptions of free persons of color was passed by the legislature, which, with secession, had other things on its mind.

Charleston Decr 23/60

Dear Henry

Finding it not practicable to leave on 24th you may expect me on 25th. I expect to bring something for Isaac[1] from Fanny,[2] which may be an inducement for him to bring the cart to the Depot.

The demonstrations in honor of Secession are not yet over.[3] It is very diverting, especially to children who do not look to the consequences. The Commissioners elect R W Barnwell,[4] J H Adams[5] & J L Orr[6] are to proceed forthwith to Washington. It is feared there will be no Congress as the Republicans are leaving so as to prevent a Quorum tomorrow when the South Carolina Delegation were to withdraw & it is probable they will not return to meet the Commissioners from the Convention of So Ca.[7]

One of the bills came up & is postponed. The others will no doubt lay over until after the adjournment.[8]

I have pledged the Stateburgians,[9] Your Father especially, as he directed me to do so, to a movement on foot to send out 2 persons to select a place or report on certain places where the people may emigrate as it is now a fixed fact that we must go. I hope it will meet the sanction & support of us all. Our situation is not only unfortunate but deplorable & it is better to make a sacrifice now than wait to be sacrificed *our selves*. To use Mr Saml. Weston's[10] language, "There has been too *much* deliberation already." Now he is like the Sumterian[11] you tell of. He never had the first notion before. Old Jake[12] confers with me very often now & he is of the same mind. I will see you soon I hope when we can confer freely.

Do have Caesar[13] to patch the book I send. It was bursted in drawing on & I may not be able to get it done here tomorrow being blue Monday[14] & Christmas Eve at that. Father & the Family yours in Love.

Do mention to your Father about the emigration. As ever yrs in haste.

J M Johnson

Mr. H. Ellison

1. A slave of William Ellison, Sr. See letters of December 28, 1858, note 1 and February 25, 1860, note 1, above.

2. Isaac's mother; see letter of October 12, 1848, note 1, above. James D. Johnson's letter of December 28, 1858, above, mentioned that Isaac's parents were in Charleston.

3. A large parade composed of militia units, fire companies, vigilance societies, bands, and other citizens had thronged the

streets of Charleston on Friday, December 21, celebrating secession with speeches, music, rockets, and roman candles. Charleston *Mercury*, December 22, 1860.

4. Robert Woodward Barnwell, one of the three commissioners appointed to go to Washington to negotiate for possession of the Charleston forts, was born in 1801 near Beaufort and served in the South Carolina legislature and in the United States House of Representatives and Senate. A delegate to the Southern Congress in Montgomery in February 1861, he went on to represent South Carolina in the Confederate Senate. *Dictionary of American Biography*, s.v. "Barnwell, Robert."

5. James Hopkins Adams was born in 1812 in Richland District and served as governor of South Carolina, in both houses of the state legislature, and in the United States House of Representatives. He died shortly after returning from his mission to Washington. Ibid., s.v. "Adams, James."

6. James Lawrence Orr was born in 1822 in Pendleton District and became a member of the South Carolina legislature, governor of the state, and in 1848 a member of the United States Congress, where in 1857 he was elected speaker of the House of Representatives. Elec-

ted to the Senate of the Confederacy in 1861, he served until Richmond fell. He became governor of South Carolina again during President Andrew Johnson's Reconstruction. Ibid., s.v. "Orr, James."

7. The overheated political atmosphere of Charleston made it difficult to come by accurate news from Washington, and Johnson's garbled report illustrates that difficulty. There was no Republican boycott of Congress; in fact, both the Committee of Thirteen in the Senate and the Committee of Thirty-three in the House met throughout the latter part of December to deal with the problems of secession. In addition, South Carolina's three commissioners were going to Washington to meet with President Buchanan, not members of Congress. The commissioners arrived in Washington on December 26, but because of Major Robert Anderson's surprise move from Fort Moultrie to Fort Sumter, they were not able to meet with Buchanan until December 28. They presented a formal demand that the government transfer all federal property in Charleston harbor to newly independent South Carolina. After some vacillation, Buchanan announced on New Year's Day that the federal government would turn over no property and would instead

maintain its troops wherever they were garrisoned. Warning Buchanan that he would bear the responsibility for the war that was coming, the commissioners returned to Charleston. Nichols, *The Disruption of American Democracy*, 397–434; Potter, *Lincoln and His Party*, 253–55; Stampp, *And the War Came*, 59–79.

8. Indeed, as Johnson's father predicted in his letter of December 19, above, none of the laws directed at free people of color was passed by the state legislature.

9. The free colored community in Stateburg.

10. The prominent free colored tailor; see letter of September 3, 1860, note 2, above.

11. A free person of color in Sumter District who, like Samuel Weston, had never before considered emigration.

12. Jacob Weston, Samuel Weston's brother and partner in the tailor shop on Queen Street. See letters of June 25, 1855, note 2 and December 7, 1860, note 16, above.

13. Caesar was a slave who belonged to William Ellison, Sr. Inventory of the Estate of William Ellison, December 21, 1861, William Ellison Estate Papers, Box 151, Package 8, Sumter County Estate Papers, SCDAH.

14. Workingmen often took it easy on Mondays, if they worked at all. The tradition of using Monday as a day of transition between the weekend and the work week was widespread among urban working men in mid-nineteenth-century America and Europe. Mathews, *A Dictionary of Americanisms*, 146.

Charles[ton] Decr 9th, 61

Dear Friend

[*torn page*] with feelings of the Deepest condolence [in y]our recent affliction in the loss of my Esteemed friend your father.[1] I take
up my pen to write you these few lines hoping they may find you
enjoying the Blessing of health and all of family also. I was in hopes
of seeing your Dear Father before he breathed his last in this world,
but alas! little did I think that I would have been deprived of the
pleasure. The will of Lord must be done. Remember me to your
Brother William and all of the family and that I deeply simpathise
with them in their affliction. My Wife is deeply Distressed on account of the death of your Father and with the exciting times down
here on account of the war,[2] that I am almost afraid she will become
distracted & therefore am very sorry but I am compelled to send you
some things for her by the R.R. to day. I hope you will receive them
for me in good order as I send them. Nothing more at present & remain your Esteemed friend

J. D. Johnson

1. On December 5, 1861, at
the age of seventy-one, William
Ellison died. He was buried in
the family cemetery in Stateburg. He had not left South
Carolina during the enslavement crisis of the previous winter, nor, with the exception of
the children of William, Jr., had
any other member of the Ellison
and Johnson families. Although
their decision to leave had been
firm, they, like other members
of the free colored elite, were
tied to the state because they
had businesses to attend to, accounts outstanding, and property to dispose of. In William
Ellison's case, the practical
problems associated with leaving would have been extreme. It
is difficult to imagine how he
could have quietly (so as not to
raise suspicions about his loyalty) disposed of sixty-three
slaves, two homes, a gin business, and over 800 acres of land,
and all between Christmas of
1860 and April 1861, when the
outbreak of the fighting closed
off the possibility of escape.
Moreover, the great fear—a
final assault on freedom itself
—never materialized. White
South Carolinians in fact quickly
lost sight of free people of color.
After the bombardment of Fort
Sumter, whites were attending
to more pressing matters.

2. A month earlier, on November 7, Union forces captured Port Royal and secured a
permanent federal stronghold
on the South Carolina coast less
than 50 miles south of Charleston. The Union victory caused

a panic in the city; a federal attack seemed imminent. By December, when Johnson wrote, the feverish preparation for the defense of the city and the tales of refugees from the captured Sea Islands made for "exciting times." Burton, *The Siege of Charleston*, 71–80; Cauthen, *South Carolina Goes to War*, 136–38.

Charleston March 23 64

My Dear Brother[1]

This will acknowledge the receipt of the corn sent for which accept my thanks and would herein express my regret that I was unsuccessful in getting the salt off to you.[2] Mr Johnson[3] apprised me about sunset of his intentions to go to Stateburgh, and I had just gone to see Martha[4] at the time. I returned home a little after dark, and started immediately to his house, requesting him to call in the morning for the salt. He said it would be out of his power to stop, as he was going up King St road.[5] I returned home and strove my best to get a dray but it was too late. I could not succeed. In the morning before day Mr J sent the drayman that took his things, but I had not the bags prepared, in consequence of his indecision. I however trust God willing to get up there in about 3 or 4 weeks time and if that time will suit, I will bring it up myself.

I hope you are well and that your Brother has recovered. Your kind Sister[6] and our Dear Tilda,[7] I hope are quite well. Mr Weston[8] was quite indisposed when I left the country. The girls[9] are both well together with myself. I am sorry to inform you of the Death of our Friend Mr Jacob Weston, who Died last night of Paralysis.

I am truly sorry to learn that Jane[10] was sent home in the manner described. I am surprised at Frances,[11] she is well when I was there last and Martha[12] as usual. Excuse this scrall and believe me as ever

your sister
Louisa P Weston

1. Henry Ellison was the brother-in-law of Louisa P. Weston; see letter of October 12, 1848, note 6, above.

2. The detailed yearly returns of the William Ellison estate reveal that throughout the war Henry and William Ellison, Jr., produced large quantities of food crops on the family lands around Stateburg. From time to time, they sold substantial amounts of corn, bacon, syrup and fodder to the Confederate government. They also sold provisions to white planters in the neighborhood. Family members in Charleston, such as Louisa Weston, also received food from their relatives in Stateburg. William Ellison Estate Papers, Box 151, Package 8, Sumter County Estate Papers, SCDAH.

3. Probably James M. Johnson but possibly his father, James D. Johnson.

4. Probably Louisa P. Weston's sister, Martha S. (Bonneau) Wilson, who married James Wilson according to an informant of E. Horace

Fitchett. Fitchett, "Free Negro in Charleston," 48.

5. The wagon road up the Charleston peninsula that led, eventually, to Stateburg.

6. Eliza Ann Johnson, James M. Johnson's wife.

7. Matilda Ellison, Henry's daughter and Louisa Weston's niece.

8. Louisa P. Weston's husband, Furman (or Faman) Weston. It has proved impossible to determine his whereabouts in the country.

9. Louisa P. Weston's daughters, Mary and Jeannette. 1860 Population Schedules, Charleston, Ward 5, dwelling 188, SCDAH.

10. Probably Louisa P. Weston's niece, Jane Holloway, the daughter of Frances P. (Bonneau) Holloway. See letter of February 14, 1852, note 4, above.

11. Louisa P. Weston's sister, Frances P. (Bonneau) Holloway. See letter of February 14, 1852, note 6, above.

12. See note 4, above.

Bibliography Of Sources Cited

Manuscript Collections

Chapel Hill, North Carolina
  Southern Historical Collection
    The Borough House Papers
    Christopher Gustavus Memminger Papers (microfilm)
    Singleton Family Papers
Charleston, South Carolina
  Charleston County Courthouse
    Probate Records
  Charleston County Library
    Record of Wills, Charleston County (typescript)
  Charleston Library Society
    Charleston Free Negro Tax Book, 1862
  Grace Episcopal Church
    Parish Register
  South Carolina Historical Society
    Anne King Gregorie Papers
  Robert Scott Small Library, College of Charleston
    Holloway Scrapbook, 1811–1964
    Minutes of the Brown Fellowship Society, 1869–1911
    Minutes of the Friendly Moralist Society, 1841–1856
Columbia, South Carolina
  South Carolina Department of Archives and History
    Charleston Free Negro Tax Books, 1816–1857
    Miscellaneous Records
    Sumter County Deeds of Conveyance
    Sumter County Estate Papers
    United States Census manuscript schedules, 1850 and 1860
  South Caroliniana Library, University of South Carolina
    Burn Family Papers
    Church of the Holy Cross, Record of the Claremont Parish,
      1809–1866
    Ellison Family Papers
    Means-English-Doby Papers
    Moody Family Papers
    St. Philip's Protestant Episcopal Church, 1810–1857, Parish
      Register
Sumter, South Carolina

Sumter County Historical Society
    Sumter County Guardians of Free Blacks, 1823–1842
Ottawa, Canada
  Public Archives
    Canada West Census, 1861, Toronto (microfilm), Reels 172–80
Salt Lake City, Utah
  Genealogical Library, Church of Jesus Christ of Latter-day Saints
    Canada West Census, 1861, Brant County, Ontario (microfilm),
      Reel 79
Washington, D.C.
  Library of Congress, Manuscript Division
    James Redpath Papers (microfilm)
    Carter G. Woodson Papers (microfilm)

Contemporary Newspapers and Periodicals

Baltimore (Md.) *Sun*, 1860–1861
Charleston (S.C.) *Courier*, 1848–1864
Charleston (S.C.) *Mercury*, 1848–1864
Columbia (S.C.) *State*, 1931
Douglass' Monthly, 1860–1862
New York (N.Y.) *Tribune*, 1860–1861
Philadelphia (Pa.) *Evening Bulletin*, 1860–1861
Southern Episcopalian, 1858–1861
Sumter (S.C.) *Banner*, 1848–1851
Sumter (S.C.) *Southern Whig*, 1831
Sumter (S.C.) *Watchman*, 1860
Toronto (Can.) *Daily Globe*, 1860

Printed Primary Sources

Bacon, Benjamin C. *Statistics of the Colored People of Philadelphia*. Phila-
    delphia, 1859.
Fay, T. C. *Charleston Directory and Stranger's Guide for 1840 and 1841*.
    Charleston, 1840.
Ferslew, W. Eugene. *Directory of the City of Charleston, 1860*. Charleston,
    1860.
Ford, Frederick A. *Census of the City of Charleston, South Carolina, For the
    Year 1861*. Charleston, 1861.
Kennedy, Lionel H., and Parker, Thomas. *An Official Report of the Trial of
    Sundry Negroes, Charged with an Attempt to Raise an Insurrection in
    the State of South Carolina*. Charleston, 1822.
List of Taxpayers of the City of Charleston, 1859. Charleston, 1860.
List of the Taxpayers of the City of Charleston, 1860. Charleston, 1861.
McCord, David J., and Cooper, Thomas, eds. *The Statutes at Large of*

South Carolina; edited, Under the Authority of the Legislature. 10 vols. Columbia, S.C., 1836–1840.

Means and Turnbull [no first names given]. *The Charleston Directory [1859].* Charleston, 1859.

O'Neall, John Belton. *The Negro Law of South Carolina.* Columbia, 1848.

Prentiss, William O. *A Sermon Preached at St. Peter's Church, Charleston on Wednesday, November 21, 1860, Being a Day of Public Fasting, Humiliation, and Prayer.* Charleston, 1860.

Redpath, James, ed. *A Guide to Hayti.* Boston, 1861.

Reports and Resolutions of the General Assembly of South Carolina. Columbia, S.C., 1859.

Rules and Regulations of the Brown Fellowship Society. Charleston, 1844.

U.S. Bureau of the Census. *Eighth Census of the United States, 1860, Population.* Washington, D.C., 1864.

Walker, H. Pinckney, comp., *Ordinances of the City of Charleston From the 19th of August 1844, to the 14th of September 1854. . . .* Charleston, 1854.

Secondary Works

Adger, John B. *My Life and Times.* Richmond, Va., 1899.

Berlin, Ira. *Slaves Without Masters: The Free Negro in the Antebellum South.* New York, 1974.

Berry, Brewton. *Almost White.* New York and London, 1963.

Billington, Ray Allen, ed. *The Journal of Charlotte Forten: A Free Negro in the Slave Era.* Toronto, 1961.

Birnie, C. W. "The Education of the Negro in Charleston, South Carolina, Prior to the Civil War." *Journal of Negro History* 12 (January 1927): 13–21.

Burton, E. Milby. *The Siege of Charleston, 1861–1865.* Columbia, S.C., 1970.

Cauthen, Charles Edward. *South Carolina Goes to War, 1860–1865.* Chapel Hill, N.C., 1950.

Curry, Leonard P. *The Free Black in Urban America, 1800–1850: The Shadow of a Dream.* Chicago and London, 1981.

Davis, Edwin Adams, and Hogan, William Ransom, eds. *The Barber of Natchez: Wherein a Slave Is Freed and Rises to a Very High Standing; Wherein the Former Slave Writes a Two-Thousand-Page Journal about His Town and Himself; Wherein the Free Negro District Is Appraised in Terms of His Friends, His Code, and His Community's Reaction to His Wanton Murder.* Baton Rouge, 1954.

Degler, Carl N. *Neither Black Nor White: Slavery and Race Relations in Brazil and the United States.* New York, 1971.

Evans, W. McKee. *To Die Game: The Story of the Lowry Band, Guerrillas of Reconstruction.* Baton Rouge, 1971.

Fitchett, E. Horace. "The Free Negro in Charleston, South Carolina."
  Ph.D. dissertation, University of Chicago, 1950.

Gatewood, Willard B., Jr., ed. *Free Man of Color: The Autobiography of
  Willis Augustus Hodges*. Knoxville, Tenn., 1982.

Gregorie, Anne King. *History of Sumter County, South Carolina*. Sumter,
  S.C., 1954.

Henry, Howell Meadows. *The Police Control of the Slave in South Carolina*.
  Emory, Va., 1914.

Hogan, William Ransom, and Davis, Edwin Adams, eds. *William Johnson's
  Natchez: The Antebellum Diary of a Free Negro*. Baton Rouge, 1951.

Holt, Thomas. *Black Over White: Negro Political Leadership in South Carolina during Reconstruction*. Urbana, Chicago, and London, 1977.

Johnson, Michael P. and Roark, James L. *Black Masters: A Free Family of
  Color in the Old South*. New York and London, 1984.

———. "'A Middle Ground': Free Mulattoes and the Friendly Moralist
  Society of Antebellum Charleston." *Southern Studies* 21 (Fall 1982):
  246–65.

Lewis, Janice Sumler. "The Fortens of Philadelphia: An Afro-American
  Family and Nineteenth-Century Reform." Ph.D. dissertation, Georgetown University, 1978.

Litwack, Leon F. *North of Slavery: The Negro in the Free States,
  1790–1860*. Chicago, 1961.

McGill, Samuel D. *Narrative of Reminiscences in Williamsburg County*.
  Columbia, S.C., 1897.

Mathews, Mitford M. *A Dictionary of Americanisms on Historical Principles*. Chicago, 1951.

Mills, Gary B. *The Forgotten People: Cane River's Creoles of Color*. Baton
  Rouge and London, 1977.

Nichols, Roy Franklin. *The Disruption of American Democracy*. New York,
  1948.

Parler, Josie Platt. *The Past Blows Away: On the Road to Poinsett Park*.
  Sumter, S.C., 1939.

Pease, Jane H., and Pease, William H. *They Who Would Be Free: Blacks'
  Search for Freedom, 1830–1861*. New York, 1974.

Plowden, David. *Bridges: The Spans of North America*. New York, 1974.

Potter, David M. *The Impending Crisis, 1848–1861*. Edited and completed by Don E. Fehrenbacher. New York, 1976.

———. *Lincoln and His Party in the Secession Crisis*. New Haven and
  London, 1942.

———. *The South and the Sectional Conflict*. Baton Rouge, 1968.

Rogers, George C., Jr. *Charleston in the Age of the Pinckneys*. Norman,
  Okla., 1969.

Smith, H. Shirley. *The World's Great Bridges*. New York, 1953.

Stampp, Kenneth M. *And the War Came*. Baton Rouge, 1950.

Steinman, David B., and Watson, Sara Ruth. *Bridges and Their Builders*.
  New York, 1957.

Sumter, Thomas S. *Dedicated to the Past, the Present, and the Future Inhabitants of Stateburg.* 2nd ed. Sumter, S.C., 1949.

Sweat, Edward Forrest. "Free Negroes in Antebellum Georgia." Ph.D. dissertation, Indiana University, 1957.

Taylor, George Rogers, and Neu, Irene. *The American Railroad Network, 1861–1890.* Cambridge, Mass., 1956.

Thomas, Albert Sidney. *A Historical Account of the Protestant Episcopal Church in South Carolina, 1820–1957.* Columbia, S.C., 1957.

Whitten, David O. *Andrew Durnford: A Black Sugar Planter in Antebellum Louisiana.* Natchitoches, La., 1981.

Wikramanayake, Marina. *A World in Shadow: The Free Black in Antebellum South Carolina*, Columbia, S.C., 1973.

Wiley, Bell I., ed. *Slaves No More: Letters from Liberia, 1833–1869.* Lexington, Ky., 1980.

Williamson, Joel. *New People: Miscegenation and Mulattoes in the United States.* New York, 1980.

Woodson, Carter G., ed. *The Mind of the Negro as Reflected in Letters Written During the Crisis 1800–1860.* Washington, D.C., 1926.

Woodward, C. Vann, ed. *Mary Chesnut's Civil War.* New Haven and London, 1981.

Index